The City-Heiress: or, Sir Timothy Treat-all. A comedy.

Aphra Behn

The BiblioLife Network

This project was made possible in part by the BiblioLife Network (BLN), a project aimed at addressing some of the huge challenges facing book preservationists around the world. The BLN includes libraries, library networks, archives, subject matter experts, online communities and library service providers. We believe every book ever published should be available as a high-quality print reproduction; printed on- demand anywhere in the world. This insures the ongoing accessibility of the content and helps generate sustainable revenue for the libraries and organizations that work to preserve these important materials.

The following book is in the "public domain" and represents an authentic reproduction of the text as printed by the original publisher. While we have attempted to accurately maintain the integrity of the original work, there are sometimes problems with the original book or micro-film from which the books were digitized. This can result in minor errors in reproduction. Possible imperfections include missing and blurred pages, poor pictures, markings and other reproduction issues beyond our control. Because this work is culturally important, we have made it available as part of our commitment to protecting, preserving, and promoting the world's literature.

GUIDE TO FOLD-OUTS, MAPS and OVERSIZED IMAGES

In an online database, page images do not need to conform to the size restrictions found in a printed book. When converting these images back into a printed bound book, the page sizes are standardized in ways that maintain the detail of the original. For large images, such as fold-out maps, the original page image is split into two or more pages.

Guidelines used to determine the split of oversize pages:

• Some images are split vertically; large images require vertical and horizontal splits.
• For horizontal splits, the content is split left to right.
• For vertical splits, the content is split from top to bottom.
• For both vertical and horizontal splits, the image is processed from top left to bottom right.

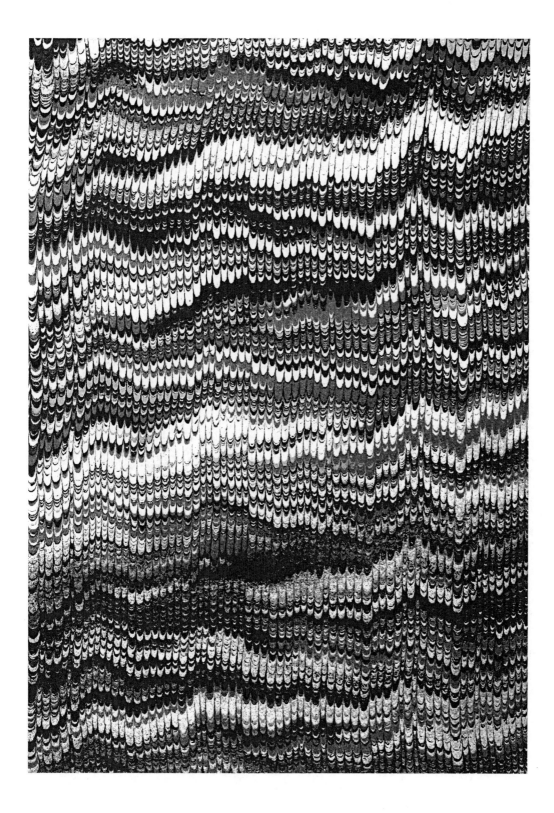

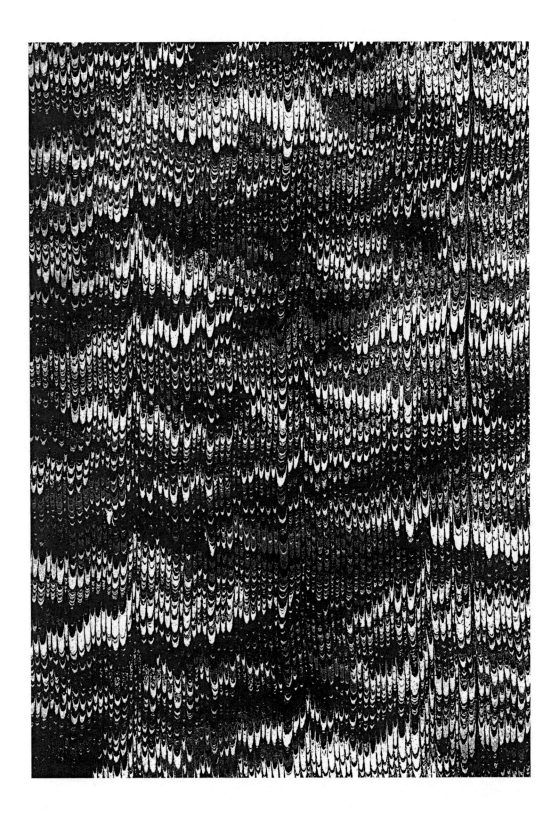

644. 9. 13

THE
CITY-HEIRESS:

OR,

Sir Timothy Treat-all.

A
COMEDY.

As it is Acted

At his Royal Highness his THEATRE.

Written by Mrs. *A. Behn.*

LONDON:

Printed for *D. Brown*, at the *Black Swan* and *Bible* without
Temple-bar ; and *T. Benskin* in *St. Brides* Church-yard ;
and *H. Rhodes* next door to the *Bear-Tavern* neer

To the Right Honourable
Henry Earl of *Arundel,* and Lord *Mowbray.*

MY LORD,

'TIs long that I have with great impatience waited some opportunity to declare my infinite Respect to your Lordship; coming, I may say, into the World with a Veneration for your Illustrious Family, and being brought up with continual Praises of the Renowned Actions of your glorious Ancestors, both in War and Peace, so famous over the Christian World for their Vertue, Piety, and Learning, their elevated Birth, and greatness of Courage, and of whom all our English History are full of the Wonders of their Lives: A Family of so ancient Nobility, and from whom so many Hero's have proceeded to bless and serve their King and Country, that all Ages and all Nations mention 'em even with Adoration. My self have been in this our Age an Eye and Ear-witness, with what Transports of Joy, with what unusual Respect and Ceremony, above what we pay to Mankind, the very Name of the Great *Howards* of *Norfolk* and *Arundel,* have been celebrated on Forein Shores! And when any one of your Illustrious Family have pass'd the Streets, the People throng'd to praise and bless him, as soon as his Name has been made known to the glad Croud. This I have seen with a Joy that became a true English heart, (who truly venerate its brave Countrymen) and joyn'd my dutiful Respects and Praises with the most devout; but never had the happiness yet of any opportunity to express particularly that Admiration I have and ever had for your Lordship and your Great Family. Still, I say, I did

A 2   admire

admire you, still I wisht and pray'd for you ; 'twas all I cou'd or durst : But as my Esteem for your Lordship dayly increas'd with my Judgment, so nothing cou'd bring it to a more absolute height and perfection, than to observe in these troublesome times, this Age of Lying, Peaching, and Swearing, with what noble Prudence, what steadiness of Mind, what Loyalty and Conduct you have evaded the Snare, that 'twas to be fear'd was laid for all the Good, the Brave, and Loyal, for all that truly lov'd our best of Kings and this distracted Country. A thousand times I have wept for fear that Impudence and Malice wou'd extend so far as to stain your Noble and ever-Loyal Family with its unavoidable Imputations ; and as often for joy, to see how undauntedly both the Illustrious Duke your Father, and your self, stem'd the raging Torrent that threatned, with yours, the ruine of the King and Kingdom ; all which had not power to shake your Constancy or Loyalty : for which, may Heaven and Earth reward and bless you ; the noble Examples to thousands of failing hearts, who from so great a President of Loyalty, became confirm'd. May Heaven and Earth bless you for your pious and resolute bravery of Mind, and heroick Honesty, when you cry'd, *Not guilty* ; that you durst, like your great self, speak Conscientious Truths in a Juncto so vitious, when Truth and Innocence was criminal : and I doubt not but the Soul of that great Sufferer bows down from Heaven in gratitude for that noble service done it. All these and a thousand marks you give of dayly growing Greatness ; every day produces to those like me, curious to learn the Story of your Life and Actions, something that even adds a Lustre to your great Name , which one wou'd think cou'd be made no more splendid : some new Goodness, some new act of Loyalty or Courage, comes out

to

to cheer the World and those that admire you. Nor wou'd I be the last of those that dayly congratulate and celebrate your rising Glory; nor durst I any other way approach you with it, but this humble one, which carries some Excuse along with it.

Proud of the opportunity then, I most humbly beg your Lordships Patronage of a Comedy, which has nothing to defend it, but the Honour it begs; and nothing to deserve that Honour, but its being in every part true Tory! Loyal all-over! except one Knave, which I hope no body will take to himself; or if he do, I must e'en say, with *Hamlet*,

----*Then let the strucken Deer go weep*----

It has the luck to be well receiv'd in the Town; which (not from my Vanity) pleases me, but that thereby I find Honesty begins to come in fashion again, when Loyalty is approv'd, and Whigism becomes a Jest where'er 'tis met with. And no doubt on't, so long as the Royal Cause has such Patrons as your Lordship, such vigorous and noble Supporters, his Majesty will be great, secure and quiet, the Nation flourishing and happy, and seditious Fools and Knaves that have so long disturb'd the Peace and Tranquility of the World, will become the business and sport of Comedy, and at last the scorn of that Rabble that fondly and blindly worshipt 'em; and whom nothing can so well convince as plain Demonstration, which is ever more powerful and prevailent than Precept, or even Preaching it self. If this have edifi'd effectual, 'tis all I wish; and that your Lordship will be pleas'd to accept the humble Offering, is all I beg, and the greatest Glory I care shou'd be done,

MY LORD,

Your Lordships most Humble
and most Obedient Servant,

A. BEHN.

THE
PROLOGUE,

Written by Mr. *Otway*.

SPOKEN by Mrs. BARRY.

HOW *vain have prov'd the Labours of the Stage,*
In striving to reclaim a vitious Age !
Poets may write the Mischief to impeach,
You care as little what the Poets teach,
As you regard at Church what Parsons preach.
But where such Follies and such Vices reign,
What honest Pen has patience to refrain ?
At Church, in Pews, ye most devoutly snore,
And here, got dully drunk, ye come to roar ;
Ye go to Church to glout, and Ogle there,
And come to meet more lewd convenient here :
With equal Zeal ye honour either place,
And run so very evenly your Race,
T'improve in Wit just as you do in Grace.
It must be so, some Dæmon has possest
Our Land, and we have never since been blest.
T' have seen it all, or heard of its Renown,
In reverend shape it stalk'd about the Town,
Six Yeomen tall attending on its frown.
Sometimes with humble note and zealous lore,
'Twou'd play the Apostolick Function o'er :
But, Heav'n have mercy on us when it swore.

When

PROLOGUE.

Whene'er it swore, to prove the Oaths were true,
Out of its mouth at random Halters flew
Round some unwary neck, by Magick thrown,
Though still the cunning Devil sav'd its own:
For when the Inchantment could no longer last,
The subtile Pug, most dexterously uncast,
Left awful form for one more seeming pious,
And in a moment vary'd to defie us:
From silken Doctor, home-spun Ananias
Left the lewd Court, and did in City fix,
Where still by its old Arts it plays new Tricks,
And fills the heads of Fools with Politicks.
This Dæmon lately drew in many a Guest,
To part with zealous Guinny for----no Feast.
Who, but the most incorrigible Fops,
For ever doom'd in dismal Cells, call'd Shops,
To cheat and damn themselves to get their Livings,
Wou'd lay sweet Money out in Sham-Thanksgivings?
Sham-Plots you may have paid for o'er and o'er;
But who ere paid for a Sham-Treat before?
Had you not better sent your Offerings all,
Hither to us, than Sequestrators Hall?
I being your Steward, Justice had been done ye;
I cou'd have entertain'd you worth your Money.

Actors

ACTORS NAMES.

Mr. Nokes,	Sir *Timothy Treat-all*,	An old seditious Knight that keeps open house for Commonwealths-men and true blue Protestants. -----He is Uncle to *Tom Wilding*.
Mr. Betterton,	*Tom Wilding*,	A Tory.--His discarded Nephew.
Mr. Lee,	Sir *Anthony Meriwill*,	An old Tory Knight of *Devonshire*.
Mr. Williams,	Sir *Charles Meriwill*,	His Nephew, a Tory also, in love with Lady *Galliard*, and Friend to *Wilding*.
Mr. Boman,	*Dresswell*,	A young Gentleman, Friend to *Wilding*.
Mr. Jevon,	*Fopington*,	A Hanger on on *Wilding*.
	Jervice,	Man to Sir *Timothy*.
	Footmen, Musick, *&c*.	
Mrs. Barry,	Lady *Galliard*,	A rich City-Widow in love with *Wilding*.
Mrs. Butler,	*Charlot*,	The City-Heiress, in love with *Wilding*.
Mrs. Corror,	*Diana*,	Mistriss to *Wilding*, and kept by him.
Mrs. Norice,	Mrs. *Clacket*,	A City-Bawd & Puritan.
Mrs. Lee,	Mrs. *Closet*,	Woman to La. *Galliard*.

SCENE *Within the Walls of London*

THE
CITY-HEIRESS:
OR,
Sir Timothy Treat-all.

ACT the First.

SCENE the First. *The Street.*

Enter Sir Timothy Treat-all, *followed by* Tom Wilding, *bare ,* Sir Charles Meriwill, Fopington, *and* Footman *with a Cloak.*

Sir Tim. TRouble me no more : for I am resolv'd, deaf and obdurate, d'ye see, and so forth.

Wild. I beseech ye, Uncle, hear me.

Sir Tim. No.

Wild. Dear Uncle———— *Sir Tim.* No.

Wild. You will be mortifi'd———— *Sir Tim.* No.

Wild. At least hear me out, Sir.

Sir Tim. No, I have heard you out too often, Sir, till you have talkt me out of many a fair thousand ; have had ye out of all the Bayliffs, Serjeants, and Constables clutches about Town, Sir ; have brought ye out of all the Surgeons, Apothecaries, and Pocky Doctors hands, that ever pretended to cure incurable Diseases ; and have crost ye out of the Books of all the Mercers, Silk-men, Exchange-men, Taylors, Shoemakers, and Sem-stristes ; with all the rest of the unconscionable City-tribe of the long Bill, that had but Faith enough to trust, and thought me Fool enough to pay.

Sir Char. But, Sir, consider, he's your own Flesh and Bloud.

Sir Tim. That's more than I'll swear.

Sir Char. Your onely Heir.

Sir Tim. That's more than you or any of his wise Associates can tell, Sir.

B *Sir*

Sir Char. Why his wife Aſſociates ? have you any exception to the Company he keeps ? This reflects on me and young *Dreſſwell,* Sir, men both of Birth and Fortune.

Sir Tim. Why, good Sir *Charles Meriwill,* let me tell you, ſince you'll have it out, That you and young *Dreſſwell* are able to debauch, deſtroy, and confound all the young imitating Fops in Town.

Sir Char. How, Sir !

Sir Tim. Nay, never huff, Sir ; for I have ſix thouſand pound a year, and value no man : Neither do I ſpeak ſo much for your particular, as for the Company you keep, ſuch Tarmagant Tories as theſe, [*to Foping.*] who are the very Vermine of a young Heir, and for one Tickling give him a thouſand Bites.

Fop. Death ! meaning me, Sir?

Sir Tim. Yes, you, Sir. Nay, never ſtare, Sir ; I fear you not : no mans hectoring ſignifies this----in the City, but the Conſtable's ; no body dares be ſawcy here, except it be in the Kings name.

Sir Char. Sir, I confeſs he was to blame.

Sir Tim. Sir *Charles,* thanks to Heaven, you may be lewd, you have a plentiful Eſtate, may whore, drink, game, and play the Devil ; your Uncle Sir *Anthony Meriwill* intends to give you all his Eſtate too : But for ſuch Sparks as this, and my Fop in faſhion here, why with what Face, Conſcience, or Religion, can they be lewd and vitious, keep their Wenches, Coaches, rich Liveries, and ſo forth, who live upon Charity, and the Sins of the Nation ?

Sir Char. If he have Youthful Vices, he has Vertues too.

Sir Tim. Yes, he had ; but I know not, you have bewitcht him amongſt ye [*weeping.*] Before he fell to Toryiſm, he was a ſober civil Youth, and had ſome Religion in him, wou'd read ye Prayers night and morning with a laudable voice, and cry *Amen* to 'em ; 'twou'd have done ones heart good to have heard him : ---- Wore decent Cloaths ; was drunk but upon Faſting-nights, and ſwore but on Sundays and Holy-days : and then I had hopes of him.   [*Still weeping.*

Wild. Aye, Heaven forgive me.

Sir Char. But, Sir, he's now become a new man, is caſting off all his Women, is drunk not above five or ſix times a week, ſwears not above once in a quarter of an hour, nor has not gam'd this two days. ----

Sir Tim. 'Twas becauſe the Devil was in's Pocket then.

Sir Char. ----Begins to take up at Coffee-houſes, talks gravely in the City, ſpeaks ſcandalouſly of the Government, and rails moſt abominably againſt the Pope and the French King.

Sir Tim. Aye, aye, this ſhall not wheedle me out of one Engliſh Guinny ; and ſo I told him yeſterday.

Wild. You did ſo, Sir.

Sir Tim. Yes ; by a good token you were witty upon me, and ſwore I lov'd and ho-nour'd the King nowhere but on his Coin.

Sir Char. Is it poſſible, Sir ?

Wild. God forgive me, Sir ; I confeſs I was a little overtaken.

Sir Tim. Aye, ſo it ſhou'd ſeem : for he miſtook his own Chamber, and went to bed to my Maids.

Sir Char. How ! to bed to your Maids ! Sure, Sir, 'tis ſcandal on him.

Sir

Sir Tim. No, no, he makes his brags on't, Sir. Oh that crying fin of Boafting! Well fare, I fay, the days of old *Oliver*; he by a wholfome Act, made it death to boaft; fo that then a man might whore his heart out, and no body the wifer.

Sir Char. Right, Sir, and then the men pafs'd for fober religious perfons, and the women for as demure Saints----

Sir Tim. Aye, then there was no fcandal; but now they do not onely boaft what they do, but what they do not.

Wild. I'll take care that fault fhall be mended, Sir.

Sir Tim. Aye, fo will I, if Poverty have any feats of Mortification; and fo farewel to you, Sir. [*going.*

Wild. Stay, Sir, are you refolved to be fo cruel then, and ruine all my Fortunes now depending?

Sir Tim. Moft religioufly----

Wild. You are?

Sir Tim. I am.

Wild. Death, I'll rob.

Sir Tim. Do and be hang'd.

Wild. Nay, I'll turn Papift.

Sir Tim. Do and be damn'd.

Sir Char. Blefs me, Sir, what a fcandal would that be to the Family of the *Treat-all's*!

Sir Tim. Hum! I had rather indeed he turn'd Turk or Jew, for his own fake; but as for fcandalizing me, I defie it: my Integrity has been known ever fince Forty One; I bought three thoufand a year in Bifhops Lands, as 'tis well known, and loft it at the Kings return; for which I'm honour'd by the City. But for his farther fatisfaction, confolation, and diftruction, know, That I Sir *Timothy Treat-all*, Knight and Alderman, do think my felf young enough to marry, d'ye fee, and will wipe your Nofe with a Son and Heir of my own begetting, and fo forth. [*going away.*

Wild. Death! marry!

Sir Char. Patience, dear *Tom*, or thou't fpoil all.

Wild. Damn him, I've loft all Patience, and can diffemble no longer, though I lofe all,------Very good, Sir; heark ye, I hope fhe's young and handfome; or if fhe be not, amongft the numerous lufty-ftomacht Whigs that dayly nofe your publick Dinners, fome may be found that either for Money, Charity, or Gratitude, may requite your Treats. You keep open houfe to all the Party, not for Mirth, Generofity, or good Nature, but for Roguery. You cram the Brethren, the pious City-Gluttons, with good Cheer, good Wine, and Rebellion in abundance, gormandizing all Comers and Goers, of all Sexes, Sorts, Opinions, and Religions, young half-witted Fops, hot-headed Fools, and Malecontents: You guttle and fawn on all, and all in hopes of debauching the Kings Liege-people into Commonwealths-men; and rather than lofe a Convert, you'll pimp for him. Thefe are your nightly Debauches.----Nay, rather than you fhall want it, I'll cuckold you my felf in pure Revenge.

Sir Tim. How! Cuckold his own natural Uncle!

Sir Char. Oh, he cannot be fo prophane.

Wild. Prophane! why he deni'd but now the having any fhare in me; and therefore 'tis lawful. I am to live by my wits, you fay, and your old rich good-natur'd

Cuckold

Cuckold is as fure a Revenue to a handfome young Cadet, as a thoufand pound a year. Your tolerable face and fhape is an Eftate in the City, and a better Bank than your Six *per Cent.* at any time.

Sir Tim. Well, Sir, fince Nature has furnifht you fo well, you need but up and ride, fhow and be rich; and fo your Servant, witty Mr. *Wilding.* [*Goes out, he looks after him.*

Sir Char. Whilft I am labouring anothers good, I quite neglect my own. This curfed, proud, difdainful Lady *Galliard*, is ever in my head; fhe's now at Church, I'm fure, not for Devotion, but to fhew her Charms, and throw her Darts amongft the gazing Crowd, and grows more vain by Conqueft. I'm near the Church, and muft ftep in, though it coft me a new Wound. [*Wild. ftands paufing.*

Wild. I am refolv'd-----Well, dear *Charles*, let's fup together to night, and contrive fome way to be reveng'd of this wicked Uncle of mine. I muft leave thee now, for I have an affignation here at Church.

Sir Char. Hah! at Church!

Wild. Aye, *Charles*, with the deareft fhe-Saint, and I hope finner.

Sir Char. What at Church? Pox, I fhall be difcovered now in my Amours. That's an odde place for Love-Intrigues.

Wild. Oh, I am to pafs for a fober difcreet perfon to the Relations; but for my Miftrifs, fhe's made of no fuch fanctified Materials; fhe is a Widow, *Charles*, young, rich, and beautiful.

Sir Char. Hah! if this fhould prove my Widow now! [*Afide.*

Wild. And though at her own difpofe, yet is much govern'd by Honour, and a rigid Mother, who is ever preaching to her againft the Vices of Youth, and t'other end of the Town Sparks; dreads nothing fo much as her Daughters marrying a villanous Tory: So the young one is forc'd to diffemble Religion, the beft Mask to hide a kind Miftrifs in.

Sir Char. This muft be my Lady *Galliard.* [*Afide.*

Wild. There is at prefent fome ill underftanding between us; fome damn'd Honourable Fop lays fiege to her, which has made me ill received; and I having a new Intrigue elfewhere, return her cold difdain, but now and then fhe croffes my Heart too violently to refift her. In one of thefe hot fits I now am, and muft find fome occafion to fpeak to her.

Sir Char. By Heaven, it muft be fhe! ----I am ftudying now, amongft all our fhe-Acquaintance, who this fhou'd be.

Wild. Oh, this is of quality to be conceal'd: but the deareft lovelieft Hypocrite, white as Lillies, fmooth as Rufhes, and plump as Grapes after fhowers, haughty her Meen, her Eyes full of difdain, and yet bewitching fweet; but when fhe loves, foft, witty, wanton, all that charms a Soul, and but for now and then a fit of Honour! Oh, damn the Nonfence, wou'd be all my own.

Sir Char. 'Tis fhe, by Heaven! [*afide.*] Methinks this Widow fhou'd prove a good Fortune to you, as things now ftand between you and your Uncle.

Wild. Ah, *Charles*, but I am otherways difpos'd of. There is the moft charming young thing in nature fallen in love with this perfon of mine, a rich City-Heirefs, *Charles*; I have her in poffeffion.

Sir Char. How can you love two at once? I've been as wild, and as extravagant,

as

as Youth and Wealth cou'd render me; but ne'er arriv'd to that degree of Lewdness, to deal my Heart about : my Hours I might, but Love should be intire.

Wild. Ah, *Charles*, two such bewitching Faces wou'd give thy Heart the lye : But Love divides us, and I must into Church. Adieu till night.

Sir Char. And I must follow to resolve my heart in what it dreads to learn. Here, my Cloak. [*Takes his Cloak from his man, and puts it on.*] Hah, Church is done! See, they are coming forth!

> *Enter People cross the Stage, as from Church ; amongst 'em Sir* Anthony Meriwill, *follow'd by Sir* Tim. Treat-all.

Hah, my Uncle! He must not see me here. [*Throws his Cloak over his face.*

Sir Tim. What my old Friend and Acquaintance, Sir *Anthony Meriwill*!

Sir Anth. Sir *Timothy Treat-all*!

Sir Tim. Whe! How long have you been in Town, Sir?

Sir Anth. About three days, Sir.

Sir Tim. Three days, and never came to dine with me! 'tis unpardonable! What, you keep close to the Church, I see: You are for the Surplice still, old Orthodox you : the Times cannot mend you, I see.

Sir Anth. No, nor shall they mar me, Sir.

Sir Char. They are discoursing; I'll pass by. [*Aside. Exit Sir* Char.

Sir Anth. As I take it, you came from Church too.

Sir Tim. Aye, needs must, when the Devil drives. I go to save my Bacon, as they say, once a month; and that too, after the Porrage is serv'd up.

Sir Anth. Those that made it, Sir, are wiser than we. For my part, I love good wholsome Doctrine, that teaches Obedience to my King and Superiours, without railing at the Government, and quoting Scripture for Sedition, Mutiny, and Rebellion. Why here was a jolly Fellow this morning made a notable Sermon. By *George*, our Country-Vicars are meer Scholars to your Gentlemen Town-Parsons! Hah, how he handled the Text, and run Divisions upon't! 'twou'd make a man sin with moderation, to hear how he claw'd away the Vices of the Town, Whoring, Drinking, and Conventicling, with the rest of the deadly number.

Sir Tim. Good lack! an he were so good at Whoring and Drinking, you'd best carry your Nephew, Sir *Charles Meriwill*, to Church ; he wants a little Documentizing that way.

Sir Anth. Hum! You keep your old wont still ; a man can begin no discourse to you, be it of *Prester John*, but you still conclude with my Nephew.

Sir Tim. Good Lord! Sir *Anthony*, you need not be so purty ; what I say, is the Discourse of the whole City, how lavishly you let him live, and give ill Examples to all young Heirs.

Sir Anth. The City! the City's a grumbling, lying, dissatisf'd City, and no wise or honest man regards what it says. Do you, or any of the City, stand bound to his Scrivener or Taylor? He spends what I allow him, Sir, his own ; and you're a Fool or Knave, chuse ye whether, to concern your self.

Sir Tim. Good lack! I speak but what wiser men discourse.

Sir Anth. Wiser men! wiser Coxcombs. What, they wou'd have me train my Nephew up, a hopeful Youth, to keep a Merchants Book, or send him to chop Logick in a University, and have him return an errant learned Ass, to simper, and look demure,

mure, and ftart at Oaths and Wenches, whilft I fell his Woods, and grant Leafes; and laftly, to make good what I have cozen'd him of, force him to marry Mrs. *Crump*, the ill-favour'd Daughter of fome Right Worfhipful. ---- A Pox of all fuch Guardians.

Sir Tim. Do, countenance Sin and Expences, do.

Sir Anth. What fin, what expences ? He wears good Cloaths, why Trades-men get the more by him; he keeps his Coach, 'tis for his eafe; a Miftrifs, 'tis for his pleafure; he games, 'ti for his diverfion: And where's the harm of this ? is there ought elfe you can accufe him with ?

Sir Tim. Yes; ---- a Pox upon him, he's my Rival too. [*afide.*] Why then I'll tell you, Sir, he loves a Lady.

Sir Anth. If that be a fin, Heaven help the Wicked !

Sir Tim. But I mean honourably.----

Sir Anth. Honourably ! Why do you know any Infirmity in him, why he fhou'd not marry ?   [*Angrily.*

Sir Tim. Not I, Sir.

Sir Anth. Not you, Sir ? why then you're an Afs, Sir. ---- But is the Lady young and handf me ?

Sir Tim. Aye, and rich too, Sir.

Sir Anth. No matter for Money, fo fhe love the Boy.

Sir Tim. Love him ! no, Sir, fhe neither does, nor fhall love him.

Sir Anth. How, Sir, nor fhall love him ! By *George*, but fhe fhall, and lie with him too, if I pleafe, Sir.

Sir Tim. How, Sir ! lie with a rich City-widow, and a Lady, and to be married to a fine Reverend old Gentleman within a day or two ?

Sir Anth. His name, Sir, his name ; I'll difpatch him prefently.   [*Offers to draw.*

Sir Tim. How, Sir, difpatch him ! ---- Your Servant, Sir.   [*Offers to go.*

Sir Anth. Hold, Sir ! by this abrupt departure, I fancy you the Boy's Rival: Come, draw.   [*Draws.*

Sir Tim. How, draw, Sir !

Sir Anth. Aye draw, Sir : Not my Nephew have the Widow !

Sir Tim. With all my foul, Sir; I love and honour your Nephew. I his Rival ! alas, Sir, I'm not fo fond of Cuckoldom. Pray, Sir, let me fee you and Sir *Charles* at my houfe, I may ferve him in this bufinefs: and fo I take my leave, Sir.------ Draw quoth a ! a Pox upon him for an old Tory-rory.   [*Afide. Exit.*

Enter us from Church, Lady Galliard, Clofet, *and Footman :* Wilding *paffes carelefly by her, Sir* Charles Meriwill *following wrapt in his Cloak.*

Sir Anth. Who's here ? *Charles* muffled in a Cloak, peering after a woman ? ----My own Boy to a hair. She's handfome too. I'll ftep afide: for I muft fee the meaning on't.   [*Goes afide.*

L. Gall. Blefs me ! how unconcern'd he pafs'd !

Clof. He bow'd low, Madam.

L. Gall. But 'twas in fuch a fafhion, as expreft Indifferency, much worfe than Hate from *Wilding.*

Clof. Your Ladyfhip has us'd him ill of late; yet if your Ladyfhip pleafe, I'll call him back.

                                        L. *Gall.*

L. Gall. I'll die firſt. ---- Hah, he's going ! ---- Yet now I think on't, I have a Toy of his, which to expreſs my ſcorn, I'll give him back now : ---- this Ring.

Cloſ. Shall I carry it, Madam ?

L. Gall. You'll not expreſs diſdain enough in the delivery; and you may call him back.   [*Cloſ. goes to* Wild.

Sir Char. By Heaven, ſhe's fond of him.   [*Aſide.*

Wild. Oh, Mrs. *Cloſet !* is it you ? ---- Madam, your Servant : By this diſdain, I fear your Woman, Madam, has miſtaken her Man. Wou'd your Ladyſhip ſpeak with me ?

L. Gall. Yes. ---- But what ? the God of Love inſtruct me.   [*Aſide.*

Wild. Command me quickly, Madam : for I have buſineſs.

L. Gall. Nay, then I cannot be diſcreet in Love.   [*Aſide.*
---Your buſineſs once was Love, nor had no idle hours
To throw away on any other thought.
You lov'd as if you'd had no other Faculties,
As if you'd meant to gain Eternal Bliſs
By that Devotion onely : And ſee how now you're chang'd.

Wild. Not I, by Heaven ; 'tis you are onely chang'd.
I thought you'd love me too, curſe on the dull miſtake ;
But when I beg'd to reap the mighty Joy
That Mutual Love affords,
You turn'd me off for Honour,
That nothing fram'd by ſome old ſullen Maid,
That wanted Charms to kindle flames when young.

Sir Anth. By *George*, he's i'th' right.   [*Aſide.*

Sir Char. Death ! can ſhe hear this Language ?   [*Aſide.*

L. Gall. How dare you name this to me any more ?
Have you forgot my Fortune, and my Youth ?
My Quality, and Fame ?

Wild. No, by Heaven, all theſe increaſe my Flame.

L. Gall. Perhaps they might, but yet I wonder where
You got the boldneſs to approach me with it.

Wild. Faith, Madam, from your own encouragement.

L. Gall. From mine ! Heavens, what contempt is this !

Wild. When firſt I paid my Vows, (good Heaven forgive me)
They were for Honour all ;
But wiſer you, thanks to your Mothers care too,
Knowing my Fortune an uncertain hope,
My Life of ſcandal, and my lewd Opinion,
Forbid my Wiſh that way : 'Twas kindly urg'd ;
You cou'd not then forbid my Paſſion too,
Nor did I ever from your Lips or Eyes,
Receive the cruel ſentence of my Death.

Sir Anth. Gad, a fine fellow this !

L. Gall. To ſave my life, I wou'd not marry thee.

Wild. That's kindly ſaid ;

But

But to fave mine, thou't do a kinder thing;
---I know thou wo't.

   L. Gall. What, yield my Honour up!
And after find it facrific'd anew,
And made the fcorn of a triumphing Wife!

   Sir Anth. Gad, fhe's i'th' right too; a noble Girl I'll warrant her.

   L. Gall. But you difdain to fatisfie thofe fears;
And like a proud and haughty Conquerer,
Demand the Town, without the leaft Conditions.

   Sir Char. By Heaven, fhe yields apace.   [*Afide.*

   Sir Anth. Pox on't, wou'd I'd ne'er feen her; now have I a Legend of fmall
Cupids at Hot-cockles in my heart.

   Wild. Now am I pawfing on that word Conditions.
Thou fayft thou wou'dft not have me marry thee;
That is, as if I lov'd thee for thy Eyes,
And put 'em out to hate thee:
Or like our Stage-fmitten Youth, who fall in love with a woman for Acting finely,
and by taking her off the Stage, deprive her of the onely Charm fhe had,
Then leave her to Ill Luck.

   Sir Anth. Gad, he's i'th' right again too! A rare Fellow!

   Wild. For, Widow, know, hadft thou more Beauty, yet not all of 'em were half
fo great a Charm as thy not being mine.

   Sir Anth. Hum! How will he make that out now?

   Wild. The ftealths of Love, the Midnight kind admittance,
The gloomy Bed, the foft-breath'd murmuring Paffion;
Ah, who can guefs at Joys thus fnatcht by parcels!
The difficulty makes us always wifhing,
Whilft on thy part, Fear ftill makes fome refiftance;
And every Bleffing feems a kind of Rape.

   Sir Anth. H'as don't! ---- A Divine Fellow this; juft of my Religion. I am ftudying now whether I was never acquainted with his Mother.

                    L. Gall. *walks away,* Wild. *follows.*

   L. Gall. Tempt me no more! What dull unwary Flame
Poffeft me all this while! Confufion on thee,   [*In Rage.*
And all the Charms that dwell upon thy Tongue.
Difeafes ruine that bewitching form,
That with thy foft feign'd Vows debaucht my Heart.

   Sir Char. Heavens! can I yet endure!   [*Afide.*

   L. Gall. By all that's good, I'll marry inftantly;
Marry, and fave my laft ftake, Honour, yet,
Or thou wilt rook me out of all at laft.

   Wild. Marry! thou canft not do a better thing:
There are a thoufand Matrimonial Fops,
Fine Fools of Fortune,
Good-natur'd Blockheads too, and that's a wonder.

   L. Gall. That will be manag'd by a man of Wit.

                                  Wild.

Wild. Right.

L. Gall. I have an eye upon a Friend of yours.

Wild. A Friend of mine! then he muſt be my Cuckold.

Sir Char. Very fine! can I endure yet more?   [*Aſide.*

L. Gall. Perhaps it is your Uncle.

Wild. Hah, my Uncle!   [*Sir* Charles *makes up to 'em.*

Sir Anth. Hah, my *Charles!* why well ſaid *Charles,* he bore up briskly to her.

Sir Char. Ah, Madam, may I preſume to tell you----

Sir Anth. Ah, Pox, that was ſtark naught! he begins like a Fore-man o'th' Shop,
to his Maſters Daughter.

Wild. How, *Charles Meriwill* acquainted with my Widow!

Sir Anth. Why do you wear that ſcorn upon your face?
I've nought but honeſt meaning in my Paſſion;
Whilſt him you favour, ſo prophanes your Beauties,
In ſcorn of Marriage and religious Rites,
Attempts the ruine of your ſacred Honour.

L. Gall. Hah, *Wilding,* boaſt my love!   [*Aſide.*

Sir Anth. The Devil take him, my Nephew's quite ſpoil'd!
Why what a Pox has he to do with Honour now?

L. Gall. Pray leave me, Sir.

Wild. Damn it, ſince he knows all, I'll boldly own my flame---
You take a liberty I never gave you, Sir.

Sir Char. How, this from thee! nay, then I muſt take more,
And ask you where you borrow'd that Brutality,
T'approach that Lady with your ſawcy Paſſion.

Sir Anth. Gad, well done, *Charles!* here muſt be ſport anon.

Wild. I will not anſwer every idle Queſtion.

Sir Char. Death, you dare not.

Wild. How, dare not!

Sir Char. No, dare not: for if you did----

Wild. What durſt you, if I did?

Sir Char. Death, cut your Throat, Sir.   [*Taking hold on him roughly.*

Sir Anth. Hold, hold, let him have fair play, and then curſe him that parts ye.
                    Taking 'em aſunder, they draw.

L. Gall. Hold, I command ye, hold!

Sir Char. There reſt my Sword to all Eternity.   [*Lays his Sword at her feet.*

L. Gall. Now I conjure ye both, by all your Honour,
If you were e'er acquainted with that Vertue,
To ſee my face no more,
Who durſt diſpute your intereſt in me thus,
As for a common Miſtriſs, in your Drink.
          She goes out, and all but Wild. *Sir* Anth. *and Sir* Char.
                    who ſtands ſadly looking after her.

Sir Anth. A heavenly Girl!---- Well, now ſhe's gone, by *George,* I am for diſpu-
ting your Title to her by dint of Sword.

Sir Char. I wo'not fight.

                    C   *Wild.*

Wild. Another time we will decide it, Sir.   [*Wild goes out.*

Sir Anth. After your whining Prologue, Sir, who the Devil would have expected such a Farce ? --- Come, *Charles*, take up thy Sword, *Charles* ; --- and, d'ye hear, forget me this Woman. ---

Sir Char. Forget her, Sir ! there never was a thing so excellent !

Sir Anth. You lye, Sirrah, you lye, there are a thousand
As fair, as young, and kinder, by this day,
We'll into th' Country, *Charles*, where every Grove
Affords us Rustick Beauties,
That know no Pride nor Painting,
And that will take it and be thankful, *Charles* ;
Fine wholsome Girls that fall like ruddy Fruit,
Fit for the gathering, *Charles*.

Sir Char. Oh, Sir, I cannot relish the coarse Fare.
But what's all this, Sir, to my present Passion ?

Sir Anth. Passion, Sir ! you shall have no Passion, Sir.

Sir Char. No Passion, Sir ! shall I have life and breath ?

Sir Anth. It may be not, Sirrah, if it be my will and pleasure.
---Why how now ! sawcy Boys be their own Carvers ?

Sir Char. Sir, I am all Obedience.   [*Bowing and sighing:*

Sir Anth. Obedience ! Was ever such a Blockhead ! Why then if I command it, you will not love this Woman ?

Sir Char. No, Sir.

Sir Anth. No, Sir ! But I say, Yes, Sir, love her me ; and love her me like a man too, or I'll renounce ye, Sir.

Sir Char. I've try'd all ways to win upon her heart,
Presented, writ, watcht, fought, pray'd, kneel'd, and weept.

Sir Anth. Why there's it now ; I thought so : Kneel'd and weept ! a Pox upon thee---I took thee for a prettier fellow.---
You shou'd a hufft and bluster'd at her door ;
Been very impudent and sawcy, Sir ;
Lewd, ruffling, mad ; courted at all hours and seasons ;
Let her not rest, nor eat, nor sleep, nor visit.
Believe me, *Charles*, women love importunity.
Watch her close, watch her like a Witch, Boy,
Till she confess the Devil in her, ---Love.

Sir Char. I cannot, Sir.
Her Eyes strike such an awe into my Soul,---

Sir Anth. Strike such a Fiddlestick.---Sirrah, I say, do't ; what, you can towse a Wench as handsomly---You can be lewd enough upon occasion. I know not the Lady, nor her Fortune ; but I am resolv'd thou shalt have her, with practising a little Courtship of my mode.---Come---

Come, my Boy *Charles*, since you must needs be doing,
I'll shew thee how to go a Widow-wooing.

ACT

ACT the Second.

SCENE the First. *A Room.*

Enter Charlot, Fopington, and Clacket.

Charl. ENough, I've heard enough of *Wilding's* Vices, to know I am undone. [*weeps*] ---*Galliard* his Miſtriſs too? I never ſaw her, but I have heard her fam'd for Beauty, Wit, and Fortune.
That Rival may be dangerous.

Fop. Yes, Madam, the fair, the young, the witty Lady *Galliard*, even in the height of all his love to you; nay, even whilſt his Uncle courts her for a Wife, he deſignes himſelf for a Gallant.

Charl. Wonderous Inconſtancy and Impudence!

Mrs. Clack. Nay, Madam, you may rely upon Mr. *Fopington's* Information : therefore if you reſpect your Reputation, retreat in time.

Charl. Reputation! that I forfeited when I ran away with your Friend Mr. *Wilding.*

Mrs. Clack. Ah, that ever I ſhould live to ſee [*weeps*] the ſole Daughter and Heir of Sir *Nicholas Gettall*, run away with one of the lewdeſt Heathens about town!

Charl. How! your Friend Mr. *Wilding* a Heathen; and with you too, Mrs. *Clacket*! That Friend Mr. *Wilding*, who thought none ſo worthy as Mrs. *Clacket*, to truſt with ſo great a ſecret as his flight with me; he a Heathen!

Mrs. Clack. Aye, and a poor Heathen too, Madam. 'Slife, if you muſt marry a man to buy him Breeches, marry an honeſt man, a religious man, a man that bears a Conſcience, and will do a woman ſome Reaſon.---Why here's Mr. *Fopington*, Madam; here's a Shape, here's a Face, a Back as ſtraight as an Arrow, I'll warrant.

Charl. How! buy him Breeches! Has *Wilding* then no Fortune?

Fop. Yes, Faith, Madam, pretty well; ſo, ſo, as the Dice run : and now and then he lights upon a Squire, or ſo, and between fair and foul Play, he makes a ſhift to pick a pretty Livelihood up.

Charl. How! does his Uncle allow him no preſent Maintenance?

Fop. No, nor future Hopes neither : Therefore, Madam, I hope you will ſee the difference between him and a man of Parts, that adores you. [*Smiling and bowing.*

Charl. If I find all this true you tell me, I ſhall know how to value my ſelf and thoſe that love me.
---This may be yet a Raſcal.

Enter Maid.

Maid. Miſtriſs, Mr. *Wilding's* below. [*Exit.*

Fop. Below! Oh, Heavens, Madam, do not expoſe me to his lewd fury, for being too zealous in your ſervice. [*In great diſorder.*

Charl. I will not let him know you told any thing, Sir.

C 2   *Fop.*

Fop. Death! to be feen here, would expofe my Life. [*To* Clacket.

Mrs. *Clack.* Here, here, ftep out upon the Sair-cafe, and flip into my Chamber.
         Going out, returns in fright.

Fop. 'Owns, he's here! lock the door faft ; let him not enter.

Mrs. *Clack.* Oh, Heavens, I have not the Key ! hold it, hold it faft, fweet, fweet Mr. *Foping* Oh, fhould there be Murder done, what a fcandal wou'd that be to the houfe of a true Proteftant ! [*Knocks.*

Charl. Heavens ! what will he fay and think, to fee me fhut in with a man ?

Mrs. *Clack.* Oh, I'll fay you're fick, afleep, or out of humour.

Charl. I'd give the world to fee him. [*Knocks.*

Wild. [*Without.*] *Charlot, Charlot* ! Am I deny'd an entrance ? By Heaven, I'll break the door. [*Knocks again ;* Fop. *ftill holding it.*

Fop. Oh, I'm a dead man, dear *Clacket* ! [*Knocking ftill.*

Mrs. *Clack.* Oh, hold, Sir, Mrs. *Charlot* is very fick.

Wild. How, fick, and I kept from her !

Mrs. *Clack.* She begs you'll come again an hour hence.

Wild. Delay'd, by Heaven I will have enterance.

Fop. Ruin'd! undone ! for if he do not kill me, he may ftarve me.

Mrs. *Clack.* Oh; he will break in upon us ! Hold, Sir, hold a little ; Mrs. *Charlot* is juft—juft--fhifting her felf, Sir : you will not be fo uncivil as to prefs in, I hope, at fuch a time.

Charl. I have a fine time on't between ye, to have him think I am ftripping my felf before Mr. *Fopington.*----Let go, or I'll call out and tell him all.

 Wild. *breaks open the door and rufhes in :* Fop. *ftands clofe up at the enterance till he is paft him, then venturing to flip out, finds* Wild. *has made faft the door ; fo he is forc'd to return again and ftand clofe up behind* Wild. *with figns of fear.*

Wild. How now, *Charlot,* what means this new unkindnefs? What, not a word ?

Charl. There is fo little Mufick in my Voice, you do not care to hear it ; you have been better entertain'd, I find, mightily employ'd, no doubt.

Wild. Yes Faith, and fo I have, *Charlot* : Damn'd Bufinefs, that Enemy to Love, has made me rude.

Charl. Or that other Enemy to Love, damn'd Wenching.

Wild. Wenching! how ill haft thou tim'd thy Jealoufie ! What Banker, that to morrow is to pay a mighty fum, wou'd venture out his ftock to day in little parcels, and lofe his Credit by it ?

Charl. You wou'd, perfidious as you are, though all your Fortune, all your future Health, depended on that Credit. [*Angry.*

Wild. So : Heark ye, Mrs. *Clacket,* you have been prating I find in my abfence, giving me a handfome character to *Charlot.* ---You hate any good thing fhould go by your own Nofe. [*Afide, to* Clacket.

Mrs. *Clack.* By my Nofe, Mr. *Wilding* ! I defie you : I'd have you to know, I fcorn any good thing fhou'd go by my Nofe in an uncivil way.

Wild. I believe fo.

Mrs. *Clack.* Have I been the Confident to all your fecrets this three years, in ficknefs and in health, for richer, for poorer ; conceal'd the nature of your wicked Difeafes,under the honeft name of Surfeits ; call'd your filthy Surgeons, Mr. Doctor,

                   to

to keep up your Reputation ; civilly receiv'd your tother-end-of-the-Town young Relations at all hours ; ---

Wild. High !

Mrs. *Clack.* Been up with you and down with you early and late, by night and by day ; let you in at all hours, drunk and sober, single and double; and civilly withdrawn, and modestly shut the door after me ?

Wild. Whir ! The storm's up, and the Devil cannot lay it.

Mrs. *Clack.* And am I thus rewarded for my pain !   [*Weeps.*

Wild. So Tempests are allay'd by showers of Rain.

Mrs. *Clack.* That I shou'd be charg'd with speaking ill of you, so honest, so civil a Gentleman---

Charl. No, I have better witness of your falshood.

Fop. Hah, 'sdeath, she'll name me !

Wild. What mean you, my *Charlot ?*
Do you not think I love you ?

Charl. Go ask my Lady *Galliard,* she keeps the best account of all your Sighs and Vows,
And robs me of my dearest softer hours.   [*Kindly to him.*

Mrs. *Clack.* You cannot hold from being kind to him.   [*Aside.*

Wild. Galliard! How came she by that secret of my life ? [*aside.*] Why Aye, 'tis true, I am there sometimes about an Arbitration, about a Suit in Law, about my Uncle.

Charl. Aye, that Uncle too---
You swore to me you were your Uncles Heir ;
But you perhaps may chance to get him one,
If the Lady prove not cruel.

Wild. Death and the Devil, what Rascal has been prating to her !   [*Aside.*

Charl. Whilst I am reserv'd for a dead lift, if Fortune prove unkind, or wicked Uncles refractory,
Yet I cou'd love you, though you were a Slave,   [*In a soft tone to him.*
And I were Queen of all the Universe.

Mrs. *Clack.* Aye, there you spoil'd all again---you forget your self.

Charl. And all the world, when he looks kindly on me.
But I'll take courage, and be very angry.   [*Aside.*
Nor does your Perjuries rest here ; you're equally as false to *Galliard,* as to me ; false for a little Mistriss of the Town, whom you've set up in spight to Quality.   [*Angry.*

Mrs. *Clack.* So, that was home and handsome.

Wild. What damn'd Informer does she keep in Pension ?

Charl. And can you think my Fortune and my Youth
Merits no better Treatment ?   [*Angry.*
How cou'd you have the heart to use me so ?   [*Soft to him.*
I fall insensibly to Love and Fondness.   [*Aside.*

Wild. Ah, my dear *Charlot !* you who know my heart, can you believe me false ?

Charl. In every Syllable, in every Look :
Your Vows, your Sighs, and Eyes, all counterfeit ;
You said you lov'd me, where was then your truth ?

You

You swore you were to be your Uncle's Heir :
Where was your confidence of me the while,
To think my Generosity so scanted,
To love you for your Fortune ?
---How every look betrays my yielding heart!   [*Aside.*
No, since men are grown so cunning in their
Trade of Love, the necessary Vice I'll practice too,
And chaffer with Love-Merchants for my Heart.
Make it appear you are your Uncles Heir,
I'll marry ye to morrow.
Of all thy Cheats, that was the most unkind,
Because you thought to conquer by that Lye.
---To night I'll be resolv'd.

  Wild. Hum! to night !

  Charl. To night, or I will think you love me for my Fortune ; which if you find elsewhere to more advantage,
I may unpitied die---and I should die,
If you should prove untrue.   [*Tenderly to him.*

  Mrs. *Clack.* There you've dasht all again.

  Wild. I am resolv'd to keep my credit with her ; ---Here's my hand :
This night, *Charlot*, I'll let you see the Writings.
---But how, a Pox of him that knows for *Thomas.*   [*Aside.*

  Charl. Hah, that Hand without the Ring !
Nay, never study for a handsome Lye.

  Wild. Ring! Oh, aye, I left it in my Dressing-room this morning.

  Charl. See how thou hast inur'd thy Tongue to Falshood !
Did you not send it to a certain Creature
They call *Diana*,
From off that hand that plighted Faith to me?

  Wild. By Heaven, 'tis Witchcraft all,
Unless this Villain *Fopington* betray me.
Those sort of Rascals will do any thing
For ready Meat and Wine.---I'll kill the Fool---Hah, here !

  Fop. Here, Lord ! Lord !   [*Turns quick and sees him behind him.*
Where were thy Eyes, dear *Wilding* ?

  Wild. Where they have spy'd a Rascal.
Where was this Property conceal'd ?

  Fop. Conceal'd ! What dost thou mean, dear *Tom* ? Why I stood as plain as the Nose on thy Face, mun.

  Wild. But 'tis the ungrateful quality of all your sort, to make such base returns.
How got this Rogue admittance, and when in,
The Impudence to tell his treacherous Lyes ?

  Fop. Admittance ! Why thou'rt stark mad : Did not I come in with you, that is, followed you ?

  Wild. Whither?

  Fop. Why into the house, up stairs, stood behind you when you swore you wou'd come in, and followed you in.   *Wild.*

Wild. All this, and I not fee!

Fop. Oh, Love's blind; but this Lady faw me, Mrs. *Clacket* faw me ---Admittance quotha!

Wild. Why did you not fpeak?

Fop. Speak! I was fo amaz'd at what I heard, the villanous Scandals laid on you by fome pick-thank Rogue or other, I had no power.

Wild. Aye, thou knowſt how I am wrong'd.

Fop. Oh, moſt damnably, Sir!

Wild. Abufe me to my Miſtrifs too!

Fop. Oh, Villains! Dogs!

Charl. Do you think they've wrong'd him, Sir? for I'll believe you.

Fop. Do I think, Madam? Aye, I think him a Son of a Whore that faid it; and I'll cut's Throat.

Mrs. Clack. Well, this Impudence is a heavenly Vertue!

Wild. You fee now, Madam, how Innocence may fuffer.

Charl. In fpight of all thy villanous diffembling, I muſt believe, and love thee for my quiet.

Wild. That's kind; and if before to morrow I do not ſhew you I deferve your Heart, kill me at once by quitting me.--- Farewel.--- [*goes out with* Fop.] I know both where my Uncle's Will and other Writings lie, by which he made me Heir to his whole Eſtate.

My craft will be in catching; which if paſt,
Her Love fecures me the kind Wench at laſt. [*Afide.*

Mrs. Clack. What if he ſhou'd not chance to keep his word now?

Charl. How if he ſhou'd not? by all that's good, if he ſhou'd not, I am refolv'd to marry him however. We two may make a pretty ſhift with three thoufand pound a year; yet I wou'd fain be refolv'd how affairs ſtand between the old Gentleman and him. I wou'd give the world to fee that Widow too, that Lady *Galliard.*

Mrs. Clack. If you're bent upon't, I'll tell you what we'll do, Madam: There's every day mighty Feaſting here at his Uncles hard by, and you ſhall difguife your felf as well as you can, and go for a Niece of mine I have coming out of *Scotland*: there you will not fail of feeing my Lady *Galliard,* though I doubt, not Mr. *Wilding,* who is of late difcarded.

Charl. Enough; I am refolv'd upon this defigne: Let's in and and practife the Northern Dialect. *Exit both.*

SCENE the Second. *The Street.*

Enter Wilding *and* Fopington.

Wild. But then *Diana* took the Ring at laſt?

Fop. Greedily; but rail'd, and fwore, and ranted at your late unkindnefs, and wou'd not be appeas'd.

Enter

Enter Dreſſwell.

Wild. Dreſſwell, I was juſt going to ſee for thee.

Dreſſ. I'm glad, dear *Tom*, I'm here to ſerve thee.

Wild. And now I've found thee, thou muſt along with me.

Dreſſ. Whither? But I'll not ask, but obey.

Wild. To a kind ſinner, *Frank*.

Dreſſ. Pox on 'em all: prithee turn out thoſe petty Tyrants of thy Heart, and fit it for a Monarch, Love, dear *Widling*, of which thou never knewſt the pleaſure yet, or not above a day.

Wild. Not knew the pleaſure! Death, the very Eſſence, the firſt draughts of Love: Ah, how pleaſant 'tis to drink when a man's adry! The reſt is all but dully ſipping on.

Dreſſ. And yet this *Diana*, for thither thou art going, thou haſt been conſtant to this three or four years.

Wild. A conſtant Keeper thou meanſt; which is indeed enough to get the ſcandal of a Coxcomb: But I know not, thoſe ſort of Baggages have a kind of Faſcination ſo inticing---and Faith, after the Fatigues of Formal Viſits to a mans dull Relations, or what's as bad, to women of Quality; after the buſie Afflictions of the Day, and the Debauches of the tedious Night, I tell thee, *Frank*, a man's beſt Retirement is with a ſoft kind Wench. But to ſay truth, I have a farther deſigne in my Viſit now. Thou knowſt how I ſtand paſt hope of Grace, excommunicated the Kindneſs of my Uncle.

Dreſſ. True.

Wild. My lewd Debauches, and being o'th' wrong Party, as he calls it, is now become an reconcilable Quarrel; ſo that I having many and hopeful Intrigues now depending, eſpecially theſe of my charming Widow, and my City-Heireſs, which can by no means be carri'd on without that damn'd Neceſſary call'd Ready Money, I have ſtretcht my Credit, as all young Heirs do, till 'tis quite broke. Now Liveries, Coaches, and Cloaths muſt be had, they muſt, my Friend.

Dreſſ. Why doſt thou not in this Extremity clap up a Match with my Lady *Galliard*? or this young Heireſs you ſpeak of?

Wild. But Marriage, *Frank*, is ſuch a Bug-bear! And this old Uncle of mine may one day be gathered together, and ſleep with his Fathers, and then I ſhall have ſix thouſand pound a year, and the wide World before me; and who the Devil cou'd reliſh theſe Bleſſings with the clog of a Wife behind him? ---But till then, Money muſt be had, I ſay.

Fop. Aye, but how, Sir?

Wild. Why, from the old Fountain, *Jack*, my Uncle; he has himſelf decreed it: he tells me I muſt live upon my Wits, and will, *Frank*.

Fop. Gad, I'm impatient to know how.

Wild. I believe thee, for thou art out at Elboes: and when I thrive, you ſhow i'th' Pit, behind the Scenes, and Coffee-houſes. Thy Breeches give a better account of my Fortune, than *Lilly* with all his Schemes and Stars.

Fop. I own I thrive by your Influence, Sir.

Dreſſ. Well; but to your Project, Friend: to which I'll ſet a helping Hand, a Heart, a Sword, and Fortune.

Wild.

Wild. You make good what my Soul conceives of you.   Let's to *Diana* then, and there I'll tell thee all.   [*Going out, they meet* Diana, *who enters with her Maid* Betty, *and Boy; looks angrily.*

---*Diana*, I was just going to thy Lodgings!

Dian. Oh las, you are too much taken up with your rich City-Heiress.

Wild. That's no cause of quarrel between you and I, *Diana*; you were wont to be as impatient for my marrying, as I for the death of my Uncle: for your rich Wife ever obliges her Husbands Mistriss; and women of your sort, *Diana*, ever thrive better by Adultery than Fornication.

Dian. Do, try to appease the easie Fool with these fine Expectations: --- No, I have been too often flatter'd with the hopes of your marrying a rich Wife, and then I was to have a Settlement; but instead of that, things go backward with me, my Coach is vanisht, my Servants dwindled into one necessary Woman and a Boy, which to save Charges, is too small for any service; my twenty Guinnies a week, into forty Shillings: a hopeful Reformation!

Wild. Patience, *Diana*, things will mend in time.

Dian. When, I wonder? Summer's come, yet I am still in my embroider'd Manto, when I'm drest, lin'd with Velvet; 'twou'd give one a Feavor but to look at me: yet still I am flamm'd off with hopes of a rich Wife, whose Fortune I am to lavish. ---But I see you have neither Conscience nor Religion in you; I wonder what a Devil will become of your Soul for thus deluding me!   [*Weeps.*

Wild. By Heaven, I love thee!

Dian. Love me! what if you do? how far will that go at the Exchange for Poynt? Will the Mercer take it for currant Coin? ---But 'tis no matter, I must love a Wit, with a Pox, when I might have had so many Fools of Fortune: But the Devil take me, if you deceive me any longer.   [*Weeping.*

Wild. You'll keep your word, no doubt, now you have sworn.

Dian. So I will.   I never go abroad, but I gain new Conquest.   Happy's the man that can approach neerest the side-box where I sit at a Play, to look at me; but if I daign to smile on him, Lord, how the o're-joy'd Creature returns it with a bow low as the very Benches! Then rising, shakes his Ears, looks round, with pride, to see who took notice how much he was in favour with charming Mrs. *Dy.*

Wild. No more: Come, let's be Friends, *Diana*; for you and I must manage an Uncle of mine.

Dian. Damn your Projects, I'll have none of 'em.

Wild. Here, here's the best Softner of a womans heart; 'tis Gold, two hundred Pieces: Go, lay it on, till you shame Quality, into plain Silk and Fringe.

Dian. Lord, you have the strangest power of Perswasion! ---Nay, if you buy my Peace, I can afford a penyworth.

Wild. So thou canst of any thing about thee.

Dian. Well, your Project, my dear *Tommy?*

Wild. Thus then----Thou, dear *Frank*, shalt to my Uncle, tell him that Sir *Nicholas Gettall*, as he knows, being dead, and having left, as he knows too, one onely Daughter his whole Executrix, Mrs. *Charlot*, I have by my civil and modest behaviour, so won upon her heart, that two nights since she left her Fathers Countryhouse at *Lusum* in *Kent*, in spight of all her strict Guards, and run away with me.

          D   *Dress.*

Dreſſ. How, wilt thou tell him of it then?

Wild. Hear me---That I have hitherto ſecured her at a Friends houſe here in the City ; but diligent ſearch being now made, dare truſt her there no longer. And make it my humble Requeſt by you, my Friend, (who are onely privy to this ſecret) that he wou'd give me leave to bring her home to his houſe ; whoſe very Authority will defend her from being ſought for there.

Dreſſ. Aye, Sir, but what will come of this, I ſay?

Wild. Why a Settlement : You know he has already made me Heir to all he has; after his deceaſe ; but for being a wicked Tory, as he calls me, he has, after the Writings were made, ſign'd, and ſeal'd, refus'd to give 'em in truſt. Now when he ſees I have made my ſelf Maſter of ſo vaſt a Fortune, he will immediately ſurrender, that reconciles all again.

Dreſſ. Very likely ; but wo't thou truſt him with the woman, *Thomas?*

Wild. No ; here's *Diana*, who as I ſhall bedizen, ſhall paſs for as ſubſtantial an Aldermans Heireſs, as ever fell into wicked hands. He never knew the right *Charlot*, nor indeed has any body ever ſeen her but an old Aunt and Nurſe, ſhe was ſo kept up :--- And there, *Diana*, thou ſhalt have a good opportunity to lye, diſſemble, and jilt in abundance, to keep thy hand in ure. Prithee, dear *Dreſſwell*, haſte with the News to him.

Dreſſ. Faith, I like this well enough ; this Project may take, and I'll about it.
                                                               [*Goes out.*

Wild. Go, get ye home, and trick and betawder your ſelf up like a right City-Lady, rich, but ill-faſhion'd ; on with all your Jewels, but not a Patch, ye Gipſie, nor no Spaniſh Paint, d'ye hear.

Dian. I'll warrant you for my part.

Wild. Then before the old Gentleman, you muſt behave your ſelf very ſoberly, ſimple, and demure, and look as prew as at a Conventicle ; and take heed you drink not off your Glaſs at Table, nor rant, nor ſwear ; one Oath confounds our Plot, and betrays thee to be an errant Drab.

Dian. Doubt not my Art of Diſſimulation.

Wild. Go, haſte and dreſs---   [*Exit Dian. Bet. and Boy.*

   Enter *L. Gall.* and Cloſet *above in the Balcony ;* Wild. *going out, ſees them, ſtops, and reads a Paper.*

Wild. Hah, who's yonder, the Widow ! a Pox upon't, now have not I power to ſtir ; ſhe has a damn'd hank upon my Heart, and nothing but right down lying with her, will diſſolve the Charm. She has forbid me ſeeing her, and therefore I am ſure will the ſooner take notice of me.   [*Reads.*

Cloſ. What will you put on to night, Madam ? you know you are to ſup at Sir *Timothy Treat-all's.*

L. Gall. Time enough for that ; prithee let's take a turn in this Balcony, this City-garden, where we walk to take the freſh Air of the Sea-coal-ſmoak. Did the Footman go back, as I order'd him, to ſee how *Wilding* and Sir *Charles* parted?

Cloſ. He did, Madam ; and nothing cou'd provoke Sir *Charles* to fight after your Ladyſhips ſtrict Commands. Well, I'll ſwear he's the ſweeteſt natur'd Gentleman--- has all the advantages of Nature and Fortune : I wonder what Exception your Ladyſhip has to him.

                                                               L. Gall.

L. *Gall.* Some small Exception to his whining humour; but I think my chiefest dislike is, because my Relations wish it a Match between us.

It is not hate to him, but natural contradiction. Hah, is not that *Wilding* yonder? he's reading of a Letter sure.

Wild. So, she sees me. Now for an Art to make her lure me up: for though I have a greater mind than she, it shall be all her own; the Match she told me of this morning with my Uncle, sticks plaguily upon my stomach; I must break the neck on't, or break the Widows heart, that's certain. If I advance towards the door now, she frowningly retires; if I pass on, 'tis likely she may call me.   [*Advances.*

L. *Gall.* I think he's passing on,

Without so much as looking towards the window.

Clos. He's glad of the excuse of being forbidden.

L. *Call.* But, *Closet*, knowest thou not he has abus'd my fame,

And does he think to pass thus unupbraided?

Is there no Art to make him look this way?

No trick?---Prithee faign to laugh.   [*Clos. laughs.*

Wild. So, I shall not answer to that Call.

L. *Gall.* He's going! Ah, *Closet*, my Fan!--- [*Lets fall her Fan just as he passes by; he takes it up, and looks up.*] Cry mercy, Sir, I'm sorry I must trouble you to bring it.

Wild. Faith, so am I; and you may spare my pains, and send your Woman for't, I am in haste.

L. *Gall.* Then the quickest way will be to bring it.

Goes out of the Belconey with Closet.

Wild. I knew I should be drawn in one way or other.

SCENE changes to a Chamber.

Enter L. Gall. Closet *to them;* Wilding *delivers the Fan, and is retiring.*

L. *Gall.* Stay; I hear you're wonderous free of your Tongue, when 'tis let loose on me.

Wild. Who I, Widow? I think of no such trifles.

L. *Gall.* Such Railers never think when they're abusive; but something you have said, a Lye so infamous!

Wild. A Lye, and infamous of you! impossible!

What was it that I call'd you, Wife, or Honest?

L. *Gall.* How, can you accuse me for the want of either?

Wild. Yes, of both: Had you a grain of Honesty, or intended ever to be thought so, wou'd you have the impudence to marry an old Coxcomb, a Fellow that will not so much as serve you for a Cloak, he is so visibly and undeniably impotent?

L. *Gall.* Your Uncle you mean.

Wild. I do; who has not known the joy of Fornication this thirty year, and now the Devil and you have put it into his head to marry, forsooth. Oh the Felicity of the Wedding-night!

L. *Gall.* Which you, with all your railing Rhetorick, shall not have power to hinder.   D 2   *Wild.*

Wild. Not if you can help it: for I perceive you are resolv'd to be a lewd incorrigible sinner, and marryest this seditious doting fool my Uncle, onely to hang him out for the signe of the Cuckold, to give notice where Beauty is to be purchas'd, for fear otherwise we should mistake, and think thee honest.

L. Gall. So much for my want of Honesty; my Wit is the Part of the Text you are to handle next.

Wild. Let the World judge of that, by this one action: This Marriage indisputably robs you both of your Reputation and Pleasure. Marry an old Fool, because he's rich! when so many handsome proper younger Brothers wou'd be glad of you!

L. Gall. Of which hopeful number your self are one.

Wild. Who, I! Bear witness, *Closet*; take notice I'm upon my Marriage, Widow, and such a Scandal on my Reputation might ruine me: therefore have a care what you say.

L. Gall. Ha, ha, ha, Marriage! Yes, I hear you give it out, you are to be married to me: for which Defamation, if I be not reveng'd, hang me.

Wild. Yes, you are reveng'd: I had the fame of vanquishing where-e're I laid my Siege, till I knew thee, hard-hearted thee; had the honest Reputation of lying with the Magistrates Wives, when their Reverend Husbands were employ'd in the necessary Affairs of the Nation, seditiously petitioning; and then I was esteem'd; but now they look on me as a monsterous thing, that makes honourable Love to you; Oh hideous, a Husband-Lover! So that now I may protest, and swear, and lye my heart out, I find neither Credit nor Kindness; but when I beg for either, my Lady *Galliard's* thrown in my Dish: Then they laugh aloud, and cry, Who wou'd think it of gay, of fine Mr. *Wilding*! Thus the City She-wits are let loose upon me, and all for you, sweet Widow; but I am resolved I will redeem my Reputation again, if never seeing you nor writing to you more, will do it: And so farewel, faithless and scandalous honest-woman.

L. Gall. Stay, Tyrant.

Wild. I am engag'd.

L. Gall. Stay, I hear you're wondrous nice, you say.

Wild. I am, and am resolv'd to lose no more time on a peevish woman, who values her Honour above her Lover. *He goes out.*

L. Gall. Go; this is the noblest way of losing thee.

Clos. Must not I call him back?

L. Gall. No: If any honest Lover come, admit him; I will forget this Devil. Fetch me some Jewels; the company to-night at Sir *Timothy's* may divert me. [*She sits down before her Glass.*

Enter Boy.

Boy. Madam, one Sir *Anthony Meriwill* wou'd speak with your Ladyship.

L. Gall. Admit him; sure 'tis Sir *Charles* his Uncle: if he come to treat a Match with me for his Nephew, he takes me in the critical minute. Wou'd he but leave his whining, I might love him, if 'twere but in revenge.

Enter Sir Anthony Meriwill *and Sir* Charles.

Sir Anth. So, I have tutor'd the young Rogue, I hope he'll learn in time. Good day to your Ladyship; *Charles* [*putting him forward*] my Nephew here, Madam---
Sirrah---

Sirrah---notwithstanding your Ladyship's Commands---Look how he stands now, being a mad young Raskal!---Gad, he wou'd wait on your Ladyship---A Devil on him, see if he'll budge now---For he's a brisk Lover, Madam, when he once begins! A Pox on him, he'll spoil all yet.

L. Gall. Please you sit, Sir.

Sir Char. Madam, I beg your Pardon for my Rudeness.

L. Gall. Still whining?--- [*Dressing her self carelessly.*

Sir Anth. D'ye hear that, Sirrah? Oh damn it, beg Pardon! The Rogue's quite out of's part.

Sir Char. Madam, I fear my Visit is unseasonable.

Sir Anth. Unseasonable! Damn'd Rogue, unseasonable to a Widow!---Quite out.

L. Gall. There are indeed some Ladies that wou'd be angry at an untimely Visit, before they've put on their best Faces; but I am none of those that wou'd be fair in spight of Nature, Sir.---Put on this Jewel here. [*To* Clos.

Sir Char. That Beauty needs no Ornament, Heaven has been too bountiful.

Sir Anth. Heaven! Oh Lord, Heaven! a Puritanical Rogue, he courts her like her Chaplain. [*Aside vext.*

L. Gall. You are still so full of University-Complements---

Sir Anth. D'ye hear that, Sirrah?---Aye so he is, so he is indeed, Madam.---To her like a man, ye Knave. [*Aside to him.*

Sir Char. Ah, Madam, I am come!

Sir Anth. To shew your self a Coxcomb.

L. Gall. To tire me with discourses of your Passion:---Fie, how this Curl sits! [*Looking in the Glass.*

Sir Char. No, you shall hear no more of that ungrateful subject.

Sir Anth. Son of a Whore, hear no more of Love, damn'd Rogue! Madam, by *George* he lyes; he does come to speak of Love, and make Love, and to do Love; and all for Love.---Not come to speak of Love, with a Pox! 'Owns, Sir, behave your self like a man; be impudent, be sawcy, forward, bold, towzing, and lewd, d'ye hear, or I'll beat thee before her. Why what a Pox! [*Aside to him, he minds it not.*

Sir Char. Finding my hopes quite lost in your unequal Favours to young *Wilding,* I'm quitting of the Town.

L. Gall. You will do well to do so.---Lay by that Necklace; I'll wear Pearl to day. [*To* Clos.

Sir Anth. Confounded Blockhead!---By *George,* he lyes again, Madam. A Dog, I'll dis-inherit him. [*aside.*] He quit the Town, Madam! no, not whilst your Ladyship is in it, to my knowledge. He'll live in the Town, nay, in the Street where you live; nay, in the House; nay, in the very Bed, by *George*; I've heard him a thousand times swear it. Swear it now, Sirrah: Look, look, how he stands now! Why dear *Charles,* good Boy, swear a little, ruffle her, and swear Damn it, she shall have none but thee. [*aside to him.*] Why you little think, Madam, that this Nephew of mine is one of the maddest Fellows in all *Devonshire.*

L. Gall. Wou'd I cou'd see't, Sir.

Sir Anth. See't? look ye there, ye Rogue.---Why 'tis all his fault, Madam. He's seldom sober; then he has a dozen Wenches in pay, that he may with the more Authority

thority

thority break their windows. There's never a Maid within forty miles of *Meriwill*-hall to work a Miracle on, but all are Mothers. He's a hopeful Youth, I'll say that for him.

Sir Char. How I have lov'd you, my despairs shall witness: for I will die to purchase your content.   [*She rises.*

Sir Anth. Die, a damn'd Rogue! Aye, aye, I'll dis-inherit him: A Dog, die, with a Pox! No, he'll be hang'd first, Madam.

Sir Char. And sure you'll pity me when I am dead.

Sir Anth. A Curse on him; pity, with a Pox! I'll give him ne'er a Souse.

1. Gall. Give me that Essence-bottle.   [*To Clos.*

Sir Char. But for a recompence of all my sufferings---

1. Gall. Sprinkle my Handkercher with Tuberose.   [*To Clos.*

Sir Char. I beg a Favour you'd afford a stranger.

L. Gall. Sooner perhaps. What Jewel's that?   [*To Clos.*

Clos. One Sir *Charles Meriwill*---

L. Gall. Sent, and you receiv'd without my order! No wonder that he looks so scurvily. Give him the Trifle back to mend his humour.

Sir Anth. I thank you, Madam, for that repromand. Look in that Glass, Sir, and admire that sneaking Coxcomb's Countenance of yours; A Pox on him, he's past Grace, lost, gone, not a Souse, not a Groat; good buy to you, Sir. Madam, I beg your Pardon; the next time I come a wooing, it shall be for my self, Madam, and I have something that will justifie it too; but as for this fellow, if your Ladyship have e'er a small Page at leisure, I desire he may have order to kick him down stairs. A damn'd Rogue, to be civil now, when he shou'd have behav'd himself handsomely! Not an Acre, not a Shilling, ---buy, Sir Softhead. [*going out, meets* Wild. *and returns.*] Hah, who have we here, hum, the fine mad Fellow? So, so, he'll swindge him I hope; I'll stay to have the pleasure of seeing it done.

Enter Wilding, *brushes by Sir* Charles.

Wild. I was sure 'twas *Meriwill's* Coach at door.   [*Aside.*

Sir Char. Hah, *Wilding!*

Sir Anth. Aye, now Sir, here's one will waken ye, Sir.   [*To Sir* Char.

Wild. How now, Widow, you are always giving Audience to Lovers, I see.

Sir Char. You're very free, Sir.

Wild. I'm always so in the Widows Lodgings, Sir.

Sir Anth. A rare Fellow!

Sir Char. You will not do't elsewhere?

Wild. Not with so much Authority.

Sir Anth. An admirable Fellow! I must be acquainted with him.

Sir Char. Is this the Respect you pay women of her Quality?

Wild. The Widow knows I stand not much on Ceremonies.

Sir Anth. Gad, he shall be my Heir.   [*Aside still.*

L. Gall. Pardon him, Sir, this is his *Cambridge*-breeding.

Sir Anth. Aye so 'tis, so 'tis; that two years there quite spoil'd him.

L. Gall. Sir, if you've any farther business with me, speak it; if not, I'm going forth.

Sir

Sir Char. Madam, in ſhort---

Sir Anth. In ſhort to a Widow, in ſhort ! quite loſt.

Sir Char. I find you treat me ill for my Reſpect ;
And when I court you next,
I will forget how very much I love you.

Sir Anth. Sir, I ſhall be proud of your farther acquaintance ; for I like, love, and
honour you.   [*To* Wild.

Wild. I'll ſtudy to deſerve it, Sir.

Sir Anth. Madam, your Servant . A damn'd ſneaking Dog to be civil and modeſt,
with a Pox !   [*Exit Sir* Char. *and Sir* Anth.

L. Gall. See if my Coach be ready.   [*Exit* Clbſ.

Wild. Whither are you janting now ?

L. Gall. Where you dare not wait on me ; to your Uncles to Supper.

Wild. That Uncle of mine pimps for all the Sparks of his Party ;
There they all meet and bargain without ſcandal :
Fops of all ſorts and ſizes you may chuſe.
Whig-land affords not ſuch another Market.

     Enter Cloſet.

Cloſ. Madam, here's Sir *Timothy Treat-all* come to wait on your Ladyſhip to Supper.

Wild. My Uncle ! Oh, damn him, he was born to be my Plague : Not diſ-inhe-
riting me had been ſo great a diſappointment ; and if he ſees me here, I ruine all
the Plots I've laid for him. Ha, he's here !

     Enter Sir Tim.

Sir Tim. How, my Nephew *Thomas* here !

Wild. Madam, I find you can be cruel too;
Knowing my Uncle has abandon'd me.

Sir Tim. How now, Sir, what's your buſineſs here ?

Wild. I came to beg a Favour of my Lady *Galliard*, Sir, knowing her Power and
Quality here in the City.

Sir Tim. How, a Favour of my Lady *Galliard* ! The Rogue ſaid indeed he wou'd
Cuckold me. [*afide.*] Why, Sir, I thought you had been taken up with your rich
Heireſs ?

Wild. That was my buſineſs now, Sir : Having in my poſſeſſion the Daughter and
Heir of Sir *Nicholas Gettall,* I would have made uſe of the Authority of my Lady
Galliard's houſe to have ſecur'd her, till I got things in order for our Marriage ; but
my Lady, to put me off, cryes, I have an Uncle.

L. Gall. A well-contriv'd Lye.   [*Aſide.*

Sir Tim. Well, I have heard of your good Fortune ; and however a Reprobate
thou haſt been, I'll not ſhew my ſelf ſo undutiful an Uncle, as not to give the Gentlewoman a little houſe-room : I heard indeed ſhe was gone a week ago.
And, Sir, my houſe is at your ſervice.

Wild. I humbly thank you, Sir. Madam, your Servant. A Pox upon him, and
all his Aſſociation.   [*Goes out.*

Sir Tim. Come, Madam, my Coach waits below.   *Exit.*

ACT

ACT the Third.

SCENE the First.   *A Room.*

Enter Sir Timothy Treat-all *and* Jervice.

Sir Tim. HEre, take my Sword, *Jervice.* What have you inquir'd as I directed you concerning the rich Heiress, Sir *Nicholas Gettall*'s Daughter ?

Jer. Alas, Sir, inquir'd ! why 'tis all the City-News, that she's run away with one of the maddest Tories about Town.

Sir Tim. Good Lord ! Aye, aye, 'tis so ; the plaguie Rogue my Nephew has got her. That Heaven shou'd drop such Blessings in the mouths of the Wicked ! Well, *Jervice*, what Company have we in the house, *Jervice* ?

Jer. Why truely, Sir, a fine deal, considering there's no Parliament.

Sir Tim. What Lords have we, *Jervice* ?

Jer. Lords, Sir ! truly none.

Sir Tim. None ! what ne'er a Lord ! Some mishap will befal me, some dire mischance : Ne'er a Lord ! ominous, ominous ! our Party dwindles dayly. What, nor Earl, nor Marquiss, nor Duke, nor ne'er a Lord ? Hum, my Wine will lie most villanously upon my hands to night, *Jervice.* What, have we store of Knights and Gentlemen ?

Jer. I know not what Gentlemen there be, Sir ; but there are Knights, Citizens, their Wives and Daughters.

Sir Tim. Make us thankful for that ; our Meat will not lie upon our hands then, *Jervice :* I'll say that for our little *Londoners*, they are as tall fellows at a well-charg'd Board as any in *Christen lom.*

Jer. Then, Sir, there's Nonconformist-Parsons.

Sir Tim. Nay, then we shall have a cleer Board : for your true Protestant Appetite in a Lay-Elder, does a mans Table credit.

Jer. Then, Sir, there's Country-Justices and Grand-Jury-men.

Sir Tim. Well enough, well enough, *Jervice.*

Enter Mrs. Sensure.

Sen. An't like your Worship, Mr. *Wilding* is come in with a Lady richly drest in Jewels, mask'd, in his hand, and will not be deny'd speaking with your Worship.

Sir Tim. Hah, rich in Jewels ! this must be she. My Sword again, *Jervice.* ---- Bring 'em up, *Sensure.* ---- Prithee how do I look to night, *Jervice* ? [*Setting himself.*

Jer. Oh, most methodically, Sir.

Enter Wild. *and* Diana *and* Betty.

Wild. Sir, I have brought into your kind protection the richest Jewel all *London* can afford, fair Mrs. *Charlot Gettall.*

Sir Tim. Bless us, she's ravishing fair ! Lady, I had the honour of being intimate with your worthy Father. I think he has been dead----

Dian.

Dian. If he chaftize me much on that point, I fhall fpoil all. Alas, Sir, name him not; for if you do, [*weeping*] I'm fure I cannot anfwer you one Queftion.   [*Afide.*

Wild. For Heaven fake, Sir, name not her Father to her; the bare remembrance of him kills her.   [*Afide to him.*

Sir Tim. Alas, poor Soul! Lady, I beg your Pardon. How foft-hearted fhe's! I am in love; I find already a tickling kind of I know not what, run frisking through my Veins.   [*Afide.*

Betty. Aye, Sir, the good Alderman has been dead this twelvemonth juft, and has left his Daughter here, my Miftrifs, three thoufand pound a year.   [*Weeping.*

Sir Tim. Three thoufand pound a year! Yes, yes, I am in love.   [*Afide.*

Bet. Befides Money, Plate, and Jewels.

Sir Tim. I'll marry her out of hand. [*afide.*] Alas, I cou'd even weep too; but 'tis in vain. Well, Nephew, you may be gone now: for 'tis not neceffary you fhou'd be feen here, d'ye fee.   [*Pufhing him out.*

Wild. You fee, Sir, now, what Heaven has done for me; and you have often told me, Sir, when that was kind, you wou'd be fo. Thofe Writings, Sir, by which you were fo good to make me Heir to all your Eftate, you faid you wou'd put into my poffeffion, whene'er I made it appear to you I cou'd live without 'em, or bring you a Wife of Fortune home.

Sir Tim. And I will keep my word; 'tis time enough.   [*Putting him out.*

Wild. I have, 'tis true, been wicked; but I fhall now turn from my evil ways, eftablifh my felf in the religious City, and enter into the Affociation. There wants but thefe fame Writings, Sir, and your good Character of me.

Sir Tim. Thou fha't have both; all in good time, man: Go, go thy ways, and I'll warrant thee for a good Character; go.

Wild. Ay, Sir; but the Writings, becaufe I told her, Sir, I was your Heir; nay, forc'd to fwear it too, before fhe wou'd believe me.

Sir Tim. Alas, alas, how fhrewdly thou wer't put to't!

Wild. I told her too, you'd buy a Patent for me: for nothing wooes a City-Fortune like the hopes of a Ladyfhip.

Sir Tim. I'm glad of that; that I can fettle on her prefently.   [*Afide.*

Wild. You may pleafe to hint fomething to her of my Godly Life and Converfation; that I frequent Conventicles, and am drunk nowhere but at your true Proteftant Confults and Clubs, and the like.

Sir Tim, Nay, if thefe will pleafe her, I have her for certain. [*afide.*] Go, go, fear not my good word.

Wild. But the Writings, Sir.---

Sir Tim. Am I a Jew, a Turk? Thou fha't have any thing, now I find thee a Lad of Parts, and one that can provide fo well for thy Uncle.   [*Afide.*
                    Puts him out, and addreffes himfelf to the Lady.

Wild. Wou'd they were hang'd that truft you, that have but the Art of Lejerdemain, and can open the Japan-Cabinet in your Bed-chamber, where I know thofe Writings are kept. Death, what a difappointment's here! I wou'd a'fworn this Sham had paft upon him.---But, Sir, fhall I not have the Writings now?

Sir Tim. What not gone yet! for fhame, away: Canft thou diftruft thy own natural Uncle? Fie, away, *Tom,* away.

Wild. A Plague upon your damn'd Dissimulation , that never-failing Badge of all your Party, there's always mischief at the bottom on't; I know ye all; and Fortune be the Word. When next I see you, Uncle, it shall cost you dearer. *Exit.*

Enter Jervice.

Jer. An't please your Worship, Supper's almost over, and you are askt for.

Sir Tim. They know I never sup: I shall come time enough to bid 'em welcome. *Exit Jer.*

Dian. I keep you, Sir, from Supper and better Company.

Sir Tim. Lady, were I a Glutton, I cou'd be satisfi'd
With feeding on those two bright starry Eyes.

Dian. You are a Courtier, Sir; we City-maids do seldom hear such Language: in which you shew your kindness to your Nephew, more than your thoughts of what my Beauty merits.

Sir Tim. Lord, Lord, how innocent she is! [*aside.*] My Nephew, Madam? yes, yes, I cannot chuse but be wonderous kind upon his score.

Dian. Nay, he has often told me, you were the best of Uncles, and he deserves your goodness; so hopeful a young Gentleman.

Sir Tim. Wou'd I cou'd see't. [*Aside.*

Dian. So modest.

Sir Tim. Yes, ask my Maids. [*Aside.*

Dian. So civil.

Sir Tim. Yes, to my Neighbours Wives. [*aside.*] But so, Madam, I find by this high Commendations of my Nephew, your Ladyship has a very slender opinion of your devoted Servant the while; or else, Madam, with this not disagreeable face and shape of mine, six thousand pound a year, and other Vertues and Commodities that shall be nameless, I see no reason why I should not beget an Heir of my own Body, had I the helping hand of a certain victorious person in the world, that shall be nameless. [*Bowing and smirking.*

Dian. Meaning me, I am sure: If I shou'd marry him now, and disappoint my dear Inconstant with an Heir of his own begetting, 'twou'd be a most wicked Revenge for past Kindnesses. [*Aside.*

Sir Tim. I know your Ladyship is studying now who this victorious person shou'd be, whom I dare not name; but let it suffice she is, Madam, within a mile of an Oak.

Dian. No, Sir, I was considering, if what you say be true,
How unadvisedly I have lov'd your Nephew,
Who swore to me he was to be your Heir.

Sir Tim. My Heir, Madam! am I so visibly old to be so desperate?
No, I'm in my years of desires and discretion,
And I have thoughts, durst I but utter 'em;
But modestly say, Mum---

Dian. I took him for the hopefullest Gentleman---

Sir Tim. Let him hope on, so will I; and yet, Madam, in consideration of your love to him, and because he is my Nephew, young, handsome, witty, and soforth, I am content to be so much a Parent to him, as, if Heaven please,---to see him fairly hang'd.

Dian.

Dian. How, Sir!   [*In a mazie.*

Sir Tim. He has deserv'd it, Madam. First, for lampooning the Reverend City, with its noble Government, with the Right Honourable Gown-men; libelling some for Feasting, and some for Fasting, some for Cuckolds, and some for Cuckold-makers; charging us with all the seven deadly sins; the sins of our Forefathers, adding seven score more to the number; the sins of Forty One reviv'd again in Eighty One, with Additions and Amendments: for which, though the Writings were drawn by which I made him my whole Executor, I will dis-inherit him. Secondly, Madam, he deserves hanging for seducing and most feloniously bearing away a young City-Heiress.

Dian. Undone, undone! Oh with what face can I return again!
What man of Wealth or Reputation, now
Will think me worth the owning!   [*Feigns to weep.*

Sir Tim. Yes, yes, Madam, there are honest, discreet, religious and true Protestant Knights in the City, that would be proud to dignifie and distinguish so worthy a Gentlewoman.   [*Bowing and smiling.*

Bet. Look to your hits, and take fortune by the forelock, Madam.   [*Aside.*
—Alas, Madam, no Knight, and poor too!

Sir Tim. As a Tory-Poet.

Bet. Well, Madam, take comfort; if the worst come to the worst, you have Estate enough for both.

Dian. Aye, Betty, were he but honest, Betty.   [*Weeping.*

Sir Tim. Honest! I think he will not steal; but for his Body, the Lord have mercy upon't, for he has none.

Dian. 'Tis evident I am betray'd, abus'd;
H'as lookt, and sigh'd, and talkt away my Heart;
H'as sworn and vow'd, and flatter'd me to ruine.   [*Weeping.*

Sir Tim. A small fault with him; he has flatter'd and sworn me out of many a fair thousand: Why he has no more Conscience than a Politician, nor no more Truth than a Narrative (under the Rose.)

Dian. Is there no Truth nor Honesty i'th' World?

Sir Tim. Troth, very little, and that lies all i'th' City, amongst us sober Magistrates.

Dian. Were I a man, how wou'd I be reveng'd!

Sir Tim. Your Ladyship might do it better as you are, were I worthy to advise you.

Dian. Name it.

Sir Tim. Why by marrying your Ladyships most assur'd Friend, and most humble Servant, *Timothy Treat-all* of *London*, Alderman.   [*Bowing.*

Bet. Aye, this is something, Mistris; here's Reason!

Dian. But I have given my Faith and Troth to *Wilding*, Betty.

Sir Tim. Faith and Troth! We stand upon neither Faith nor Troth in the City, Lady. I have known an Heiress married and bedded, and yet with the advice of the wiser Magistrates, has been unmarried and consummated anew with another, so it stands with our Interest; 'tis Law by *Magna Charta.* Nay, had you married my ungracious Nephew, we might by this our *Magna Charta* have hang'd him for a Rape.

E 2   *Dian.*

Dian. What, though he had my confent?

Sir Tim. That's nothing, he had not ours.

Dian. Then fhou'd I marry you by ftealth, the danger wou'd be the fame.

Sir Tim. No, no, Madam, we never accufe one another ; 'tis the poor Rogues, the Tory Rafcals, we always hang.   Let 'em accufe me if they pleafe, alas, I come off hand-fmooth with *Ignoramus.*

Enter Jervice.

Jer. Sir, there's fuch calling for your Worfhip!   They are all very merry, the Glaffes go briskly about.

Sir Tim. Go, go, I'll come when all the Healths are paft; I love no Healths.

Jer. They are all over, Sir, and the Ladies are for dancing ;   fo they are all adjourning from the Dining-room hither, as more commodious for that Exercife.   I think they're coming, Sir.

Sir Tim. Hah, coming !   Call *Senfure* to wait on the Lady to her Apartment.---And, Madam, I do moft heartily recommend my moft humble Addrefs to your moft judicious confideration , hoping you will moft vigoroufly, and with all your might, maintain the Rights and Priviledges of the honourable City ; and not fuffer the force or perfwafion of any Arbitrary Lover whatfoever, to fubvert their Ancient and Fundamental Laws, by feducing and forcibly bearing away fo rich and fo illuftrious a Lady : and, Madam, we will unanimoufly ftand by you with our Lives and Fortunes. ---This I learnt from a Speech at the Election of a Burgefs.

Leads her to the door: fhe goes out with Betty *and* Senfure.

Enter Mufick playing, Sir Anthony Meriwill *dancing with a Lady in his hand, Sir* Charles *with Lady* Galliard, *feveral other women and men.*

Sir Anth. [finging.] Philander *was a jolly* Swain,
And lov'd by ev'ry Lafs ;
Whom when he met upon the Plain,
He laid upon the Grafs.

And here he kift, and there he play'd
With this, and then the tother,
Till every wanton fmiling Maid
At laft became a Mother.

And to her Swain, and to her Swain,
The Nymph begins to yield ;
Ruffle, and breathe, then to't again,
Thou'rt Mafter of the Field.

Clapping Sir *Char.* on the back.

Sir Char. And if I keep it not, fay I'm a Coward, Uncle.

Sir Anth. More Wine there, Boys, I'll keep the Humour up.

[*Enter Bottles and Glaffes.*

Sir Tim. How !   young *Meriwill* fo clofe to the Widow ! ---

Madam---

Madam----   [*Addressing himself to her,* Sir Char. *puts him by.*

Sir Char. Sir *Timothy,* why what a Pox dost thou bring that damn'd Puritanical, Schismatical, Phanatical, Small-beer-face of thine into good Company ? Give him a full Glass to the Widow's Health.

Sir Tim. O lack, Sir *Charles,* no Healths for me, I pray.

Sir Char. Heark ye, leave that couzening, canting, sanctifi'd Sneer of yours, and drink ye me like a sober loyal Magistrate, all those Healths you are behind, from his sacred Majesty, whom God long preserve, with the rest of the Royal Family, even down to this wicked Widow, whom Heaven-soon convert from her lewd designes upon my Body.   [*Pulling Sir* Tim. *to kneel.*

Sir Anth. A rare Boy ! he shall have all my Estate.

Sir Tim. How, the Widow a lewd designe upon his Body ! Nay, then I am jealous.   [*Aside.*

L. Gall. I a lewd designe upon your Body ! for what, I wonder ?

Sir Char. Why, for villanous Matrimony,

L. Gall. Who, I !

Sir Char. Who, you ? yes, you.
Why are those Eyes drest in inviting Love ?
Those soft bewitching Smiles, those rising Breasts,
And all those Charms that make you so adorable,
Is't not to draw Fools into Matrimony ?

Sir Anth. How's that, how's that ! *Charles* at his Adorables and Charms ! He must have t'other Health, he'll fall to his old Dog-trot again else. Come, come, every man his Glass. Sir *Timothy,* you are six behind. Come, *Charles,* name 'em all.   [*Each take a Glass, and force Sir* Tim. *on his knees.*

Sir Char. ----Not bate ye an Ace, Sir : Come, his Majesties Health, and Confusion to his Enemies.   [*They go to force his mouth open to drink.*

Sir Tim. Hold, Sir, hold, if I must drink, I must ; but this is very Arbitrary, methinks.   [*Drinks.*

Sir Anth. And now, Sir, to the Royal Duke of *Albany.* Musick, play a Scotch Jig.   [*Musick plays, they drink.*

Sir Tim. This is meer Tyranny.

Enter Jervice.

Jer. Sir, there is just alighted at the Gate a Person of Quality, as appears by his Train, who give him the Title of a Lord.

Sir Tim. How, a strange Lord ! Conduct him up with Ceremony, *Jervice.*----'Ods so, he's here !

Enter Wilding *in disguise,* Dresswell, *and Footmen and Pages.*

Wild. Sir, by your Reverend Aspect, you shou'd be the Renown'd *Mester de Hotell* ?

Sir Tim. Meter de Otell ! I have not the honour to know any of that name ; I am call'd Sir *Timothy Treat-all.*   [*Bowing.*

Wild. The same, Sir : I have been bred abroad, and thought all Persons of Quality had spoke French.

Sir Tim. Not City Persons of Quality, my Lord.

Wild. I'm glad on't, Sir : for 'tis a Nation I hate, as indeed I do all Monarchies.

Sir Tim. Hum ! hate Monarchy ! Your Lordship is most welcome.   [*Bows.*

Wild.

Wild. Unless Elective Monarchies, which so resemble a Commonwealth.

Sir Tim. Right, my Lord; where every man may hope to take his turn.---Your Lordship is most singularly welcome.   [*Bows low.*

Wild. And though I am a stranger to your Person, I am not to your Fame, amongst the sober Party of the *Amsterdamians*, all the French Hugonots throughout *Geneva*; even to *Hungary* and *Poland*, fames trumpet sounds your praise, making the Pope to tear, the rest admire you.

Sir Tim. I'm much oblig'd to the Renowned Mobily.

Wild. So you will say, when you shall hear my Embassie. The *Polanders* by me salute you, Sir, and have in this next new Election, prickt ye down for their succeeding King.

Sir Tim. How, my Lord, prickt me down for a King! Why this is wonderful! Prickt me, unworthy me, down for a King! How cou'd I merit this amazing Glory!

Wild. They know, he that can be so great a Patriot to his Native Country, where but a private person, what must he be when Power is on his side?

Sir Tim. Aye, my Lord, my Country, my bleeding Country! there's the stop to all my rising Greatness. Shall I be so ungrateful to disappoint this big expecting Nation? defeat the sober Party, and my Neighbours, for any Polish Crown? But yet, my Lord, I will consider on't: Mean time my House is yours.

Wild. I've brought you, Sir, the measure of the Crown: Hah, it fits you to a hair.   [*Pulls out a Ribon and measures his head.*
You were by Heaven and Nature fram'd that Monarch.

Sir Anth. Hah, at it again! [*Sir Charles making sober love.*] Come, we grow dull, *Charles*: where stands the Glass? what, balk my Lady *Galliard*'s Health!
                                        They go to drink.

Wild. Hah, *Galliard*---and so sweet on *Meriwill*!   [*Aside.*

L. Gall. If it be your business, Sir, to drink, I'll withdraw.

Sir Char. Gad, and I'll withdraw with you, Widow. Heark ye, Lady *Galliard*, I am damnably afraid you cannot bear your Liquor well, you are so forward to leave good Company and a Bottle.

Sir Tim. Well, Gentlemen, since I have done what I never do, to oblige you, I hope you'll not refuse a Health of my Denomination.

Sir Anth. We scorn to be so uncivil.   [*All take Glasses.*

Sir Tim. Why then here's a conceal'd Health that shall be nameless, to his Grace the King of *Poland*.

Sir Char. King of *Poland*! Lord, Lord, how your thoughts ramble!

Sir Tim. Not so far as you imagine; I know what I say, Sir.

Sir Char. Away with it.   [*Drink all.*

Wild. I see, Sir, you still keep up that English Hospitality that so renowned our Ancestors in History.   [*Looking on L. Gall.*

Sir Tim. Aye, my Lord, my noble Guests are my Wife and Children.

Wild. Are you not married then? Death, she smiles on him!   [*Aside.*

Sir Tim. I had a Wife, but, rest her Soul, she's dead; and I have no Plague left now, but an ungracious Nephew, perverted with Ill Customs, Tantivie-Opinions, and Court-Notions.

Wild. Cannot your pious Examples convert him?

By

By Heaven, she's fond of him! *[Aside.*

Sir Tim. Alas, I have try'd all ways, fair and foul; nay, had settled t'other day my whole Estate upon him, and just as I had sign'd the Writings, out comes me a damn'd Libel call'd, *A Warning to all good Christians against the City-Magistrates*; and I doubt he had a hand in *Absolon and Achitophel*; a Rogue: But some of our sober Party have claw'd him home, i'faith, and given him Rhyme for his Reason.

Wild. Most visibly in love! ---Oh, Sir, Nature, Laws, and Religion, plead for so neer a Kinsman.

Sir Tim. Laws and Religion! Alas, my Lord; he deserves not the name of a Patriot, who does not for the Publick Good defie all Laws and Religion.

Wild. Death, I must interrupt 'em!---Sir, pray what Lady's that? [*Wild. salutes her.*

Sir Tim. I beseech your Lordship, know her, 'tis my Lady *Galliard*: the rest are all my Friends and Neighbours, true Protestants all ----Well, my Lord, how do you like my method of doing the Business of the Nation, and carrying on the Cause with Wine, Women, and soforth?

Wild. High feeding and smart Drinking, gains more to the Party, than your smart Preaching.

Sir Tim. Your Lordship has hit it right: A rare man this!

Wild. But come, Sir, leave we serious affairs, and oblige these fair ones.

Addresses himself to Galliard, Sir Charles *puts him by.*
Enter Charlot *disguis'd* Clacket, *and* Fopington.

Charl. Heavens, *Clacket,* yonders my false one, and that my lovely Rival.

Pointing to Wild. *and* L. Gall.
Enter Diana *and* Sensure *maskt, and* Betty.

Dian. Dear Mrs. *Sensure,* this Favour has oblig'd me.

Sen. I hope you'll not discover it to his Worship, Madam.

Wild. By her meen, this shou'd be handsome.----[*Goes to* Diana.] Madam, I hope you have not made a Resolution to deny me the honour of your hand.

Dian. Hah, *Wilding!* Love can discover thee through all disguise.

Wild. Hah, *Diana!* Wou'd 'twere Felony to wear a Vizard. Gad, I'd rather meet it on the Kings Highway with Stand and Deliver, than thus encounter it on the Face of an old Mistriss; and the Cheat were more excusable. ---But how---

Talks aside with her.

Sir Char. Nay, never frown nor chide: for thus do I intend to shew my Authority, till I have made thee onely fit for me.

Wild. Is't so, my precious Uncle! are you so great a Devil in Hypocrisie! Thus had I been serv'd, had I brought him the right woman. [*Aside.*

Dian. But do not think, dear *Tommy,* I wou'd have serv'd thee so; married thy Uncle, and have cozen'd thee of thy Birthright.---But see, we're observ'd!

Charlot *listening behind him all this while.*

Charl. By all that's good, 'tis he! that Voice is his!

He going from Dian. *turns upon* Charlot *and looks.*

Wild. Hah, what pretty Creature's this, that has so much of *Charlot* in her face? But sure she durst not venture: 'tis not her dress nor meen. Dear pretty stranger, I must dance with you.

Charl. Gued deed, and see ye shall, Sir, gen you please. Tho I's not dance, Sir, I's tell ya that noo.

Wild. Nor I: so we're well matcht.   By Heaven, she's wonderous like her.

Charl. By th' Mass, not so kind, Sir :   'Twere gued that ene of us shou'd **dance** to guid the other weel.

Wild. How young, how innocent, and free she is ?
And wou'd you, fair one, be guided by me ?

Charl. In any thing that gued is.

Wild. I love you extreamly, and wou'd teach you to love.

Charl. Ah, wele aday !   [*Sighs and smiles.*

Wild. A thing I know you do not understand.

Charl. Gued faith, and ya're i'th' right, Sir ;   yet 'tis a thing I's often hear ya **gay** men talk of.

Wild. Yes, and no doubt have been told those pretty Eyes inspired it.

Charl. Gued deed, and so I have :   Ya men make sa mickle ado aboot ens Eyes, ways me, I's ene tir'd with sick-like Compliments.

Wild. Ah, if you give us Wounds, we must complain.

Charl. Ya may ene keep out a harms way then.

Wild. Oh, we cannot ; or if we cou'd, we wou'd not.

Char. Marry and I's have ene a Song tol that tune, Sir.

Wild. Dear Creature, let me beg it.

Char. Gued faith, ya shall not, Sir, I's sing without entreaty.

SONG.

Ah, Jenny, *gen your Eyes do kill,*
     You'll let me tell my pain ;
Gued faith, I lov'd against my will,
     But wad not break my Chain.
I ence was call'd a bonny Lad,
     Till that fair face if yours
Betray'd the freedom ence I had,
     And ad my bleether howers.

But noo ways me, like Winter looks,
     My gloomy showering Eyne,
And on the banks of shaded Brooks,
     I pass my wearied time.
I call the Streem that gleedeth on,
     To witness if it see,
On all the flowry Brink along,
     A Swain so true as Iee.

Wild. This very Swain am I, so true and so forlorn, unless you pity me.
This is an excellently *Charlot* wants, at least I never heard her sing.   [*Aside.*
     Sir Anth. Why *Charles*, where stands the woman, *Charles* ?

Fop. *comes up to* Charlot.

Wild. I must speak to *Galliard*, though all my Fortunes depend on the discovery

Sir Anth. Come, come, a cooling Glaſs about.

Wild. Dear *Dreſſwell,* entertain *Charles Meriwill* a little, whilſt I ſpeak to *Galliard.*

The men go all to the Drinking-table.

By Heaven, I die, I languiſh for a word!
---Madam, I hope you have not made a Vow
To ſpeak with none but that young Cavalier?
They ſay, the freedom Engliſh Ladies uſe,
Is as their Beauty, great.

L. Gall. Sir, we are none of thoſe of ſo nice and delicate a Vertue as Converſa-
tion can corrupt; we live in a cold Climate.

Wild. And think you're not ſo apt to be in love,
As where the Sun ſhines oftner.
But you too much partake of the Inconſtancy of this your fickle Climate.

Maliciouſly to her.

One day all Sun-ſhine, and th' encourag'd Lover
Decks himſelf up in glittering Robes of Hope;
And in the midſt of all their boaſted Finery
Comes a dark Cloud acroſs his Miſtriſs Brow,
Daſhes the Fool, and ſpoils the gawdy ſhow. [*L. Gall. obſerving him neerly.*

L. Gall. Hah, do not I know that railing Tongue of yours?

Wild. 'Tis from your Guilt, not Judgment then.
I was reſolv'd to be to night a Witneſs
Of that ſworn Love you flatter'd me ſo often with.
By Heaven, I ſaw you playing with my Rival,
Sigh'd, and lookt Babies in his gloating Eyes.
When is the Aſſignation? when the Hours?
For he's impatient as the raging Sea,
Looſe as the Winds, and amorous as the Sun
That kiſſes all the Beauties of the Spring.

L. Gall. I take him for a ſoberer perſon, Sir.

Wild. Have I been the Companion of his Riots
In all the lewd courſe of our early Youth,
Where like unwearied Bees we gather'd Flowers?
But no kind Bloſſome cou'd oblige our ſtay,
We rifled and were gone.

L. Gall. Your Vertues I perceive are pretty equal;
Onely his Love's the honeſter o' th' two.

Wild. Honeſter! that is, he wou'd owe his good fortune to the Parſon of the
Pariſh;
And I wou'd be oblig'd to you alone.
He wou'd have a Licenſe to boaſt he lies with you,
And I wou'd do't with modeſty and ſilence:
For Vertue's but a name kept free from Scandal,
Which the moſt baſe of women beſt preſerve,
Since Gilting and Hypocriſie cheat the world beſt.
---But we both love, and who ſhall blab the ſecret? [*In a ſoft tone.*

F *L. Gall.*

L. Gall. Oh, why were all the Charms of Speaking given to that falſe Tongue that makes no better uſe of 'em ?
--;-I'll hear no more of your inchanting Reaſons.

Wild. You muſt.

L. Gall. I will not.

Wild. Indeed you muſt.

L. Gall. By all the Powers above---

Wild. By all the powers of Love, you'll break your Oath, unleſs you ſwear this night to let me ſee you.

L. Gall. This night ?

Wild. This very night.

L. Gall. I'd die firſt.---At what hour ?   [*Firſt turns away, then ſighs and looks on him.*

Wild. Oh, name it ; and if I fail---   [*With joy.*

L. Gall. I wou'd not for the World---

Wild. That I ſhou'd fail !

L. Gall. Not name the guilty hour.

Wild. Then I through eager haſte ſhall come too ſoon,
And do your Honour wrong.

L. Gall. My Honour ! Oh that word !

Wild. Which the Devil was in me for naming.   [*Aſide.*
---At Twelve !

L. Gall. My Women and my Servants then are up.

Wild. At One, or Two.

L. Gall. So late ! 'twill be ſo quickly day !

Wild. Aye, ſo it will :
That half our buſineſs will be left unfiniſht.

L. Gall. Hah, what do you mean ? what buſineſs?

Wild. A thouſand tender things I have to ſay,
A thouſand Vows of my eternal love ;
And now and then we'll kiſs and---

L. Gall. Be extreamly honeſt.

Wild. As you can wiſh.

L. Gall. Rather as I command : for ſhou'd he know my wiſh, I were undone.
                                                         Aſide.

Wild. The Signe.---

L. Gall. Oh, preſs me not ; ---yet you may come at midnight under my Chamber-window.   [*Sir Char. ſees 'em ſo cloſe, comes to 'em.*

Sir Char. Hold, Sir, hold ! Whilſt I am liſtening to the relation of your French Fortifications, Outworks, and Counterſcarps, I perceive the Enemy in my Quarters. -- My Lord, by your leave.   [*Puts him by, growing drunk.*

Charl. Perſwade me not ; I burſt with Jealouſie.   [*Wild. turns, ſees Clacket.*

Wild. Death and the Devil, *Clacket !* then 'tis *Charlot,* and I'm diſcover'd to her.

Charl. Say, are not you a falſe diſſembling thing ?   [*To Wild. in anger.*

Wild. What, my little Northern Laſs tranſlated into Engliſh !
This 'tis to practiſe Art in ſpight of Nature.
Alas, thy Vertue, Youth, and Innocence,

                                                           Were

Were never made for Cunning,
I found ye out through all your forc'd Difguife.

Charl. Hah, did you know me then?

Wild. At the firft glance, and found you knew me too,
And talkt to yonder Lady in revenge,
Whom my Uncle wou'd have me marry. But to avoid all difcourfes of that nature,
I came to night in this difguife you fee, to be conceal'd from her; that's all.

Charl. And is that all, on honour? is it, Dear?

Wild. What, no Belief, no Faith in villanous women?

Charl. Yes, when I fee the Writings.

Wild. Go home; I die if you fhou'd be difcover'd;
And credit me, I'll bring you all you ask.

Clacket, you and I muft have an odde Reckoning about this nights jant of yours.
Afide to Clacket.

Sir Tim. Well, my Lord, how do you like our Englifh Beauties?

Wild. Extreamly, Sir; and was preffing this young Lady to give us a Song.
Here is an Italian Song in two parts.

Sir Tim. I never faw this Lady before: pray who may fhe be, Neighbour?
To Clacket.

Mrs. *Clack.* A Niece of mine, newly come out of *Scotland*, Sir.

Sir Tim. Nay, then fhe dances by nature. Gentlemen and Ladies, pleafe you to
fit, here's a young Neighbour of mine will honour us with a Dance.
They all fit; Charl. *and* Fop. *dance.*
So, fo; very well, very well. Gentlemen and Ladies, I am for Liberty of Confcience, and Moderation. There's a Banquet waits the Ladies, and my Cellars are open
to the men; but for my felf, I muft retire: firft waiting on your Lordfhip to fhew
you your Apartment, then leave you to cher entire; and to morrow, my Lord, you
and I will fettle the Nation, and refolve on what return we will make to the noble
Polanders. *Exeunt all but* Wild. Dreff. *and* Fop. Sir Char. *leading out* L. Gall.

Sir Anth. Well faid, *Charles,* thou leaveft her not, till fhe's thy own, Boy.----And
Philander *was a jolly Swain,* &c. *Exit finging.*

Wild. All things fucceed above my wifh, dear *Frank;*
Fortune is kind; and more, *Galliard* is fo:
This night crowns all my Wifhes.

Laboir, are all things ready for our purpofe? *To his Footman.*

Lab. Dark Lanthorns, Piftols, Habits and Vizards, Sir.

Fop. I have provided Portmantles to carry off the Treafure.

Dreff. I perceive you are refolv'd to make a through-ftitcht Robbery on't.

Fop. Faith, if it lie in our way, Sir, we had as good venture a Caper under the
Triple Tree for one as well as t'other.

Wild. We will confider on't. 'tis now juft ftruck Eleven: within this hour is
the dear Affignation with *Galliard.*

Dreff. What, whether our affairs be finifht or not?

Wild. 'Tis but at next door; I fhall return time enough for that trivial bufinefs.

Dreff. A trivial bufinefs of fome fix thoufand pound a year?
F 2 *Wild.*

Wild. Trivial to a woman, *Frank!* no more do you make as if you went to bed.
---*Laboire,* do you feign to be drunk, and lie on the Hall-table; and when I give the signe, let me softly in.

Dreſſ. Death, Sir, will you venture at such a time!

Wild. My life and future hope---I am resolv'd,
Let Polititians plot, let Rogues go on
In the old beaten Path of Forty One,
Let City-Knaves delight in Mutiny,
The Rabble bow to old Presbytery;
Let petty States be to confusion hurl'd,
Give me but Woman, I'll despise the World.

ACT the Fourth.

SCENE the First.   *A Dreſſing-room.*

Lady Galliard *is diſcover'd in an undreſs at her Table, Glaſs, and Toilette, Cloſet attending: As ſoon as the Scene draws off, ſhe riſes from the Table as diſturb'd and out of humour.*

L. Gall.   COme, leave your everlasting Chamber-Maids Chat, your dull Road of Slandering by rote, and lay that Paint aſide.   Thou art fuller of falſe News, than an unlicens'd Mercury.

Cloſ. I have good proof, Madam, of what I ſay.

L. Gall. Proof of a thing impoſſible !---Away.

Cloſ. Is it a thing ſo impoſſible, Madam, that a man of Mr. *Wilding's* parts and perſon ſhould get a City-Heireſs?
Such a bonne Mine, and ſuch a pleaſant Wit!

L. Gall. Hold thy fluent Tattle, thou haſt Tongue
Enough to talk an Oyſter-woman deaf; I ſay it cannot be.---
What means the panting of my troubled Heart!
Oh my preſaging fears! ſhou'd what ſhe ſays prove true,
How wretched and how loſt a thing am I!   [*Aſide.*

Cloſ. Your Honour may ſay your pleaſure; but I hope I have not liv'd to theſe years to be impertinent : --- No, Madam, I am none of thoſe that run up and down the Town a Story-hunting, and a Lye-catching, and---

L. Gall. Eternal rattle, peace! ---
Mrs. *Charlot Gettall* go away with *Wilding!*
A man of *Wilding's* extravagant life
Get a Fortune in the City!
Thou might'ſt as well have told me, a Holder forth were married to a Nun.
There are not two ſuch Contraries in Nature;
'Tis flamm, 'tis foolery, 'tis moſt impoſſible.

Cloſ. I beg your Ladyſhips pardon, if my diſcourſe offend you; but all the world knows Mrs. *Clacket* to be a perſon---   *L. Gall.*

L. Gall. Who is a moſt devout Bawd, a preciſe Procurer ;
Saint in the Spirit, and Whore in the Fleſh ;
A Doer of the Devils work in Gods Name.
Is ſhe your Informer ? nay, then the Lye's undoubted.---
I ſay once more, adone with your idle Tittle-tattle;---
And to divert me, bid *Betty* ſing the Song which *Wilding*
Made to his laſt Miſtriſs : we may judge by that
What little Haunts and what low Game he follows.
This is not like the deſcription of a rich Citizens Daughter and Heir, but ſome common Hackney of the Suburbs.

Cloſ. I have heard him often ſwear ſhe was a Gentlewoman, and liv'd with her Friends.

L. Gall. Like enough ; there are many of theſe Gentlewomen who live with their Friends, as rank Proſtitutes, as errant Jilts, as thoſe who make open profeſſion of the Trade---almoſt as mercenary---But come, the Song.   [*Enter* Betty.

SONG.

In Phillis *all vile Jilts are met,*
Fooliſh, uncertain, falſe, Coquette.
Love is her conſtant welcome Gueſt,
And ſtill the neweſt pleaſes beſt.
Quickly ſhe likes, then leaves as ſoon ;
Her life on Woman's a Lampoon.

Yet for the Plague of Humane Race,
This Devil has an Angels Face ;
Such Youth, ſuch Sweetneſs in her look,
Who can be man, and not be took ?
What former Love, what Wit, what Art,
Can ſave a poor inclining heart ?

In vain, a thouſand times an hour,
Reaſon rebels againſt her power.
In vain I rail, I curſe her Charms ;
One look my feeble Rage diſarms.
There is Inchantment in her Eyes ;
Who ſees 'em, can no more be wiſe.

Enter Wilding, *who runs to embrace* L. Gall.

Wild. Twelve was the luckie minute when we met :
Moſt charming of your Sex, and wiſeſt of all Widows,
My Life, my Soul, my Heaven to come, and here !
Now I have liv'd to purpoſe, ſince at laſt---Oh, killing Joy !---
Come, let me fold you, preſs you in my arms,
And kiſs you thanks for this dear happy night.

L. Gall. You may ſpare your thanks, Sir, for thoſe that will deſerve 'em ; I ſhall give ye no occaſion for 'em.   *Wild.*

Wild. Nay, no Scruples now, deareſt of Dears, no more ;
'Tis moſt unſeaſonable---
I bring a heart full fraight with eager hopes,
Oppreſt with a vaſt load of longing Love ;
Let me unlade me in that ſoft white Boſome,
That Store-houſe of rich Joys and laſting Pleaſures,
And lay me down as on a Bed of Lillies.   [*She breaks from him.*

L. Gall. You're wonderous full of Love and Rapture, Sir; but certainly you miſtake the perſon you addreſs 'em to.

Wild. Why, are you not my Lady *Galliard,* that very Lady *Galliard,* who if one
may take her word for't, loves *Wilding ?* Am I not come hither by your own appointment ; and can I have any other buſineſs here at this time of night, but Love,
and Rapture, and---

L. Gall. Scandalous and vain ! by my appointment, and for ſo lewd a purpoſe !
guard me, ye good Angels.
If after an Affront ſo groſs as this,
I ever ſuffer you to ſee me more,
Then think me what your Carriage calls me,
An Impudent, an open Proſtitute,
Loſt to all ſenſe of Vertue, or of Honour.

Wild. What can this mean ?   [*Aſide.*
Oh, now I underſtand the Myſtery ;   [*Looking on* Cloſet.
Her Woman's here, that troubleſome piece of Train.
---I muſt remove her.   Heark ye, Mrs. *Cloſet,* I had forgot to tell you ; As I came up I
heard a Kinſman of yours very earneſt with the Servants below, and in great haſte to
ſpeak with you.

Cloſ. A Kinſman ! that's very likely indeed, and at this time of night.

Wild. Yes, a very neer Kinſman he ſaid he was, your Fathers own Mothers Uncles Siſters Son ; what d'ye call him ?

Cloſ. Aye, what d'ye call him indeed ; I ſhou'd be glad to hear his name.   Alas,
Sir, I have no neer Relation living that I know of, the more's my misfortune, poor
helpleſs Orphan that I am.   [*Weeps.*

Wild. Nay, but Mrs. *Cloſet,* pray take me right,
This Country-man of yours, as I was ſaying---

L. Gall. Chang'd already from a Kinſman to a Country-man ! A plain contri-
vance to get my Woman out of the Room.   *Cloſet,* as you value my ſervice, ſtir
not from hence.

Wild. This Country-man of yours, I ſay, being left Executor by your Fathers
laſt Will and Teſtament, is come---Dull Waiting-woman, I wou'd be alone with your
Lady ; know your Que, and retire.

Cloſ. How, Sir !

Wild. Learn, I ſay, to underſtand Reaſon when you hear it.   Leave us a while ;
Love is not a Game for three to play at.   [*Gives her Money.*

Cloſ. I muſt own to all the world, you have convinc'd me ; I ask a thouſand Par-
dons for my dulneſs.   Well, I'll be gone, I'll run ; you're a moſt powerful perſon,
the very Spirit of Perſwaſion.--I'll ſteal out.--You have ſuch a taking way with you---
                                    But

But I forget my self.   Well, your moſt obedient Servant :   Whenever you've occaſion, Sir, be pleas'd to uſe me freely.

Wild. Nay, dear Impertinent, no more Complements, you ſee I'm buſie now ; prithee be gone, you ſee I'm buſie.

Cloſ. I'm all Obedience to you, Sir---
Your moſt obedient---

L. *Gall.* Whither are you fisking and gigiting now ?

Cloſ. Madam, I am going down, and will return immediately, immediately.

Exit Cloſ.

Wild. So, ſhe's gone ; Heaven and broad Gold be prais'd for the deliverance : And now, dear Widow, let's loſe no more pretious time ; we've fool'd away too much already.

L. *Gall.* This to me ?

Wild. To you, yes, to whom elſe ſhou'd it be ? unleſs being ſenſible you have not diſcretion enough to manage your own affairs your ſelf, you reſolve, like other Widows, with all you're worth to buy a Governour, commonly called a Husband.   I took ye to be wiſer ; but if that be your deſigne, I ſhall do my beſt to ſerve you,--- though to deal freely with you---

L. *Gall.* Trouble not your ſelf, Sir, to make Excuſes ; I'm not ſo fond of the offer to take you at your word.   Marry you ! a Rakeſhame, who have not eſteem enough for the Sex to believe your own Mother honeſt---without Money or Credit, without Land either in preſent or proſpect ; and half a dozen hungry Vices, like ſo many bawling Brats at your back, perpetually craving, and more chargeable to keep than twice the number of Children.   Beſides, I think you are provided for ; are you not married to Mrs. *Charlot Gettall ?*

Wild. Married to her ? do I know her, you ſhou'd rather ask.   What Fool has forg'd this unlikely Lye ?   But ſuppoſe 'twere true, cou'd you be jealous of a woman I marry ? do you take me for ſuch an Aſs, to ſuſpect I ſhall love my own Wife ? On the other ſide, I have a great charge of Vices, as you well obſerve, and I muſt not be ſo barbarous to let them ſtarve.   Every body in this Age takes care to provide for their Vices, though they ſend their Children a begging ; I ſhould be worſe than an Infidel to neglect them.   No, I muſt marry ſome ſtiff aukward thing or other with an ugly face and a handſome Eſtate, that's certain : but whoever is ordain'd to make my Fortune, 'tis you onely that can make me happy.---Come, do it then.

L. *Gall.* I never will.

Wild. Unkindly ſaid, you muſt.

L. *Gall.* Unreaſonable man ! becauſe you ſee
I have unuſual regards for you,
Pleaſure to hear, and trouble to deny you ;
A fatal yielding in my nature toward you,
Love bends my Soul that way.---
A weakneſs I ne'er felt for any other ;
And wou'd you be ſo baſe ? and cou'd you have the heart
To take th' advantage on't to ruine me,
To make me infamous, deſpis'd, loath'd, pointed at ?

Wild. You reaſon falſe.---
According to the ſtricteſt rules of Honour,

Beauty

Beauty fhou'd ftill be the Reward of Love,
Not the vile Merchandize of Fortune,
Or the cheap Drug of a Church-Ceremony.
She's onely infamous, who to her Bed,
For intereft, takes fome naufeous Clown fhe hates:
And though a Joynture or a Vow in publick
Be her price, that makes her but the dearer whore.

 L. Gall. I underftand not thefe new Morals.

 Wild. Have patience, I fay 'tis clear.
All the defires of mutual Love are vertuous.
Can Heaven or Man be angry that you pleafe
Your felf and me, when it does wrong to none ?
Why rave you then on things that ne'r can be ?
Befides, are we not alone, and private ? who can know it ?

 L. Gall. Heaven will know't; and I---that that's enough :
But when you're weary of me, firft your Friend, then his, then all the world.

 Wild. Think not that time will ever come.

 L. Gall. Oh, it muft, it will !

 Wild. Or if it fhou'd, cou'd I be fuch a Villain---
Ah, Cruel ! if you lov'd me as you fay,
You wou'd not thus diftruft me.

 L. Gall. You do me wrong ; I love you more than ere my Tongue,
Or all the Actions of my Life can tell you---fo well---
Your very faults, how grofs foere, to me
Have fomething pleafing in 'em.   To me you're all
That Man can praife, or, Woman can defire;
All Charm without, and all Defert within :
But yet my Vertue is more lovely ftill ;
That is a price too high to pay for you :
The love of Angels may be bought too dear,
If we beftow on them what's kept for Heaven.

 Wild. Hell and the Devil ! I'll hear no more
Of this Religious ftuff, this Godly nonfence.
Death, Madam, do you bring me into your Chamber to preach Vertue to me ?

 L. Gall. I bring you hither ! how can you fay it ?
I fuffer'd you indeed to come, but not
For the bafe end you fancy'd, but to take
A laft leave of you.   Let my heart break with Love,
I cannot be that wretched thing you'd have me :
Believe I ftill fhall have a kindnefs for you,
Always your Friend, your Miftrifs now no more.

 Wild. Cozen'd, abus'd, fhe loves fome other man !
Dull Blockhead not to find it out before !   [*Afide.*
---Well, Madam, may I at laft believe
This is your fixt and final Refolution ?
And does your Tongue now truly fpeak your Heart,
That has fo long bely'd it ?   *L. Gall.*

L. Gall. It does.

Wild. I'm glad on't. Good night: And when I visit you again, May you again thus fool me. [*Offers to go.*

L. Gall. Stay but a moment.

Wild. For what? to praise your Night-dress, or make court to your little Dog? No, no, Madam, send for Mr. *Flamfull* and Mr. *Flutterbuz*, Mr. *Lapp-fool* and Mr. *Love-all*; they'll do it better, and are more at leisure.

L. Gall. Hear me a little: You know I both despise, and hate those civil Coxcombs, as much as I esteem and love you. But why will you be gone so soon? and why are you so cruel to urge me thus to part either with your good Opinion or your Kindness? I wou'd fain keep 'em both. [*In a soft tone.*

Wild. Then keep your word, Madam.

L. Gall. My word! And have I promis'd then to be A Whore? A Whore! Oh let me think of that! A man's Convenience, his leisure hours, his Bed of Ease, To loll and tumble on at idle times; The Slave, the Hackney of his lawless Lust! A loath'd Extinguisher of filthy flames, Made use of, and thrown by.---Oh infamous!

Wild. Come, come, you love me not, I see it plain; That makes your scruples: that, that's the reason You start at words, and run away from shadows. Already some pert Fop, some Ribon-fool, Some dancing Coxcomb, has supplanted me In that unsteady treacherous woman's heart of yours.

L. Gall. Believe it if you will. Yes, let me be false, unjust, ungrateful, any thing but a---Whore---

Wild. Oh, Sex on purpose form'd to plague Mankind! All that you are, and that you do,'s a lye. False are your Faces, false your floating Hearts; False are your Quarrels, false your Reconcilements: Enemies without Reason, and Dear without Kindness. Your Friendship's false, but much more false your Love; Your damn'd deceitful Love is all o'er false.

L. Gall. False rather are the Joys you are so fond of. Be wise, and cease, Sir, to pursue 'em farther.

Wild. No, them I can never quit; but you most easily: A woman changeable, and false as you.

L. Gall. Said you most easily? Oh, inhumane! Your cruel words have wak'd a dismal thought; I feel 'em cold and heavy at my heart, And weakness steals upon my Soul apace; I find I must be miserable.--- I would not be thought false. [*In a soft tone, coming neer him.*

Wild. Nor wou'd I think you so; give me not cause.

L. Gall. What heart can bear distrust from what it loves? Or who can always her own Wish deny? [*Aside.*

And Love and Nature will at laſt o'ercome.

---Do you not then believe I love you ?   *[To him in a ſoft tone.*

Wild. How can I, while you ſtill remain unkind ?

L. *Gall.* How ſhall I ſpeak my guilty thoughts?---
I have not power to part with you : conceal my ſhame I doubt I cannot, I fear I
wou'd not any more deny you.

Wild. Oh, heavenly ſound ! Oh, charming Creature ! ſpeak that word again, a-
gen, agen ! for ever let me hear it.

L. *Gall.* But did you not indeed ? and will you never, never love Mrs. *Charlot*,
never ?

Wild. Never, never.

L. *Gall.* Turn your face away, and give me leave
To hide my riſing Bluſhes : I cannot look on you,   *As this laſt Speech is ſpeaking*
But you muſt undo me if you will.---   *ſhe ſinks into his Arms by*
Since I no other way my truth can prove,   *degrees.*
---You ſhall ſee I love.
Pity my Weakneſs, and admire my Love.

Wild. All Heaven is mine, I have it in my arms :
Nor can ill Fortune reach me any more.
Fate, I defie thee, and dull World, adieu.
In Loves kind Fever let me ever ly,
Drunk with Deſire, and raving mad with Joy.

Exeunt into the Bed-chamber, Wild. *leading her with his arms about her.*
Enter Sir Charles Meriwill *and Sir* Anthony, *Sir* Char. *drunk.*
SCENE *changes.*

Sir Anth. A Dog, a Rogue, to leave her !

Sir Char. Why look ye, Uncle, what wou'd you have a man do ?
I brought her to her Coach.---

Sir Anth. To her Coach ! to her Coach ! Did not I put her into your hand, follow'd you out, winkt, ſmil'd, and nodded ; cry'd, 'buy *Charles,* 'buy Rogue ; which
was as much as to ſay, Go home with her, *Charles,* home to her Chamber, *Charles ;*
nay, as much as to ſay, Home to her Bed, *Charles ;* nay, as much as to ſay----Hum,
hum, a Rogue, a Dog, and yet to be modeſt too ! That I ſhou'd bring thee up with
no more fear of God before my Eyes !

Sir Char. Nay, dear Uncle, don't break my heart now. Why I did proffer, and
preſs, and ſwear, and ly'd, and---but a Pox on her, ſhe has the damndeſt wheedling
way with her, as, Dear *Charles,* nay prithee, fie, 'tis late, to morrow, my Honour,
which if you lov'd, you wou'd preſerve ; and ſuch obliging Reaſons.

Sir Anth. Reaſons ! Reaſon ! a Lover, and talk of Reaſon ! You lye, Sirrah, you
lye. Leave a woman for Reaſon, when you were ſo finely drunk too, a Raſcal !

Sir Char. Why look ye, d'ye ſee, Uncle, I durſt not truſt my ſelf alone with her in
this pickle, leſt I ſhou'd a fallen foul on her.

Sir Anth. Why there's it ; 'tis that you ſhou'd adone : I am miſtaken if ſhe be not
one of thoſe Ladies that love to be raviſht of a Kindneſs. Why, your willing Rape
is all the faſhion, *Charles.*

Sir Char. But heark ye, Uncle.

Sir Anth. Why how now, Jack-ſawce, what, capitulate ?   Sir

Sir Char. Why do but hear me, Uncle: Lord, you're so hasty! Why look ye, I am as ready, d'ye see, as any man on these occasions.

Sir Anth. Are you so, Sir? and I'll make you willing, or try Toledo with you, Sir.---Whe, what, I shall have ye whining when you are sober again, traversing your Chamber with Arms across, railing on Love and Women, and at last defeated, turn whipping *Tom*, to revenge your self on the whole Sex.

Sir Char. My dear Uncle, come kiss me and be friends; I will be rul'd.[*Kisses him.*

Sir Anth. ---A most admirable good-natur'd Boy this! [*aside.*] Well then, dear *Charles*, know, I have brought thee now hither to the Widows house with a resolution to have thee order matters so, as before thou quits her, she shall be thy own, Boy.

Sir Char. Gad, Uncle, thou'rt a Cherubin! Introduce me, d'ye see, and if I do not so woo the Widow, and so do the Widow, that ere morning she shall be content to take me for better for worse.---Renounce me! Egad, I'll make her know the Lord God from *Tom Bell*, before I have done with her. Nay, backt by my noble Uncle, I'll venture on her, had she all *Cupid*'s Arrows, *Venus*'s Beauty, and *Masalina*'s Fire, d'ye see.

Sir Anth. A sweet Boy, a very sweet Boy! Hum, thou art damnable handsome to night, *Charles*.---Aye, thou wilt do't; I see a kind of a resistless Lewdness about thee, a most triumphant Impudence, loose and wanton.   [*Stands looking on him.*

Enter Closet.

Clos. Heavens, Gentlemen, what makes you here at this time of night?

Sir Char. Where's your Lady?

Clos. Softly, dear Sir.

Sir Char. Why is she asleep? Come, come, I'll wake her.

Offers to force in as to the Bed-chamber.

Clos. Hold, hold, Sir: No, no, she's a little busie, Sir.

Sir Char. I'll have no business done to night, Sweetheart.

Clos. Hold, hold, I beseech you, Sir, her Mother's with her: For Heavens sake, Sir, be gone.

Sir Char. I'll not budge.

Sir Anth. No not a foot.

Clos. The City you know, Sir, is so censorious---

Sir Char. Damn the City.

Sir Anth. All the Whigs, *Charles*, all the Whigs.

Sir Char. In short, I am resolv'd, d'ye see, to go to the Widows Chamber.

Sir Anth. Heark ye, Mrs. *Closet*, I thought I had intirely engag'd you this evening.

Clos. I am perfectly yours, Sir; but now it happens so, her Mother being there--- Yet if you wou'd withdraw for half an hour, into my Chamber, till she were gone---

Sir Anth. This is Reason, *Charles*. Here, here's two Pieces to buy thee a Gorget.

Gives her Money.

Sir Char. And here's my two, because thou art industrious.

Gives her Money, and goes out with her.

Enter

Enter Lady Galliard *in rage, held by* Wilding.

L. Gall. What have I done ? Ah, whither shall I flie ?   [*Weeps*

Wild. Why all these Tears ? Ah, why this cruel Passion ?

L. Gall. Undone, undone ! Unhand me, false, forsworn ;
Be gone, and let me rage till I am dead.
What shou'd I do with guilty Life about me ?

Wild. Why, where's the harm of what we two have done ?

L. Gall. Ah, leave me---
Leave me alone to sigh to flying Winds,
That the infection may be born aloft,
And reach no humane Ear.

Wild. Cease, lovely Charmer, cease to wound me more.

L. Gall. Shall I survive this shame! No, if I do,
Eternal Blushes dwell upon my Cheeks,
To tell the World my Crime.
---Mischief and Hell, what Devil did possess me ?

Wild. It was no Devil, but a Deity ;
A little gay-wing'd God, harmless and innocent,
Young as Desire, wanton as Summer-breezes,
Soft as thy Smiles, resistless as thy Eyes.

L. Gall. Ah, what malicious God,
Sworn Enemy to feeble Womankind,
Taught thee the Art of Conquest with thy Tongue ?
Thy false deluding Eyes were surely made
Of Stars that rule our Sexes Destiny :
And all thy Charms were by Inchantment wrought,
That first undo the heedless Gazers on,
Then shew their natural deformity.

Wild. Ah, my *Galliard*, am I grown ugly then ?
Has my increase of Passion lessen'd yours ?   [*In a soft tone.*

L. Gall. Peace tempter, Peace, who artfully betrayest me,
And then upbraidest the wretchedness thou'st made.
---Ah, Fool, eternal Fool ! to know my danger,
Yet venture on so evident a ruine.

Wild. Say,---what one Grace is faded !
Is not thy Face as fair, thy Eyes as killing ?
By Heaven, much more : This charming change of Looks,
Raises my flame, and makes me wish t'invoke
The harmless God again.   [*Embraces her.*

L. Gall. By Heaven, not all thy Art
Shall draw me to the tempting sin again.

Wild. Oh, I must, or dye.

L. Gall. By all the Powers, by---

Wild. Oh, do not swear, lest Love shou'd take it ill
That Honour shou'd pretend to give him Laws,
And make an Oath more powerful than his Godhead.

                                        ---Say

---Say that you will half a long hour hence---

L. Gall. Hah?

Wild. Or fay a tedious hour.

L. Gall. Death, never---

Wild. Or if you muft---promife me then to morrow.

L. Gall. No, hear my Vows.

Wild. Hold, fee me die; if you refolve 'em fatal to my love, by Heaven I'll do't.

         Lays his hand on his Sword.

L. Gall. Ah, what---

Wild. Revoke that fatal Never then.

L. Gall. I dare not.

Wild. Oh, fay you will.

L. Gall. Alas, I dare not utter it.

Wild. Let's in, and thou fhalt whifper it into my Bofom ; Or fighing, look it to me with thy Eyes.

L. Gall. Ah, *Wilding*---   *[Sighs.*

Wild. It toucht my Soul! Repeat that figh again.

L. Gall. Ah, I confefs I am but feeble woman.   *[Leans on him.*

Sir Char. Good Miftrifs keep-door, ftand by : for I muft enter. *[Sir Char. without.*

L. Gall. Hah, young *Meriwill's* voice !

Clof. Pray, Sir *Charles*, let me go and give my Lady notice.

        She enters and goes to Wild.

---For Heavens fake, Sir, withdraw, or my Lady's Honour's loft.

Wild. What will you have me do?   *[To* Galliard.

L. Gall. Be gone, or you will ruine me for ever.   *[In diforder.*

Wild. Nay, then I will obey.

L. Gall. Here, down the back-ftairs:---

As you have Honour, go and cherifh mine.   *[Pulling him.*

---He's gone ; and now methinks the fhivering fit of Honour is return'd.

  Enter Sir Charles, *rudely pufhing* Clofet *afide, with Sir* Anthony.

Sir Char. Deni'd an entrance! nay, then there is a Rival in the cafe, or fo ; and I'm refolv'd to difcover the Hellifh Plot, d'ye fee.

    Juft as he enters drunk at one door, Wild. *returns at the other.*

L. Gall. Ha, *Wilding* return'd! fhield me, ye Shades of Night.

      Puts out the Candles, and goes to Wild.

Wild. The back-ftairs-door is lockt.

L. Gall. Oh, I am loft! curfe on this fatal night ! Art thou refolv'd on my undoing every way?

Clof. Nay, now we're by dark, let me alone to guide you, Sir.   *[To* Wild.

Sir Char. What, what, all in darknefs? Do you make Love like Cats, by Star-light?   *[Reeling about.*

L. Gall. Ah, he knows he's here !---Oh, what a pain is Guilt !   *[Afide.*

Wild. I wou'd not be furpriz'd.

  As Clofet *takes him to lead him out, he takes out his Sword, and by dark, pufhes by Sir* Charles, *and almoft overthrows Sir* Anthony ; *at which they both draw, whilft he goes out with* Clofet.

            Sir

Sir Char. Hah, Gad 'twas a Spark! ---What, vanisht! hah---

Sir Anth. Nay, nay, Sir, I am for ye.

Sir Char. Are you so, Sir? and I am for the Widow, Sir, and---

> *Just as they are passing at each other,* Closet *enters with a Candle.*

---Hah, why what have we here,---my none flesh and blood? [*Embracing his Uncle.*

Sir Anth. Cry mercy, Sir! Pray how fell we out?

Sir Char. Out, Sir! Prithee where's my Rival? where's the Spark, the--Gad, I took thee for an errant Rival: Where, where is he?   [*Searching about.*

L. Gall. Whom seek ye, Sir, a man, and in my Lodgings?   [*Angrily.*

Clos. A man! merciful, what will this scandalous lying World come to? Here's no man.

Sir Char. Away, I say, thou damn'd Domestick Intelligence, that comest out every half hour with some fresh Sham.---No man!---What, 'twas an appointment onely, hum,--- which I shall now make bold to unappoint, render null, void, and of none effect. And if I find him here [*searches about*] I shall very civilly and accidentally, as it were, being in perfect friendship with him---pray mark that---run him through the Lungs.

L. Gall. Oh, what a Coward's guilt! what mean you, Sir?

Sir Char. Mean! why I am obstinately bent to ravish thee, thou hypocritical Widow, make thee mine by force, that so I may have no obligation to thee, and consequently use thee scurvily with a good Conscience.

Sir Anth. A most delicate Boy! I'll warrant him as lewd as the best of 'em, God grant him life and Health.   [*Aside.*

L. Gall. 'Tis late, and I entreat your absence, Sir: These are my hours of prayer, which this unseasonable Visit has disturb'd.

Sir Char. Prayer! no more of that, Sweetheart: for let me tell you, your Prayers are heard. A Widow of your Youth and Complexion can be praying for nothing so late, but a good Husband; and see, Heaven has sent him just in the crit---critical minute, to supply your occasions.

Sir Anth. A Wag, an arch Wag; he'll learn to make Lampoons presently. I'll not give sixpence from him, though to the Poor of the Parish.

Sir Char. Come, Widow, let's to bed.   [*Pulls her, she is angry.*

L. Gall. Hold, Sir, you drive the Jest too far;
And I am in no humour now for mirth.

Sir Char. Jest! Gad ye lye, I was never in more earnest in all my life.

Sir Anth. He's in a heavenly humour, thanks to good Wine, good Counsel, and good Company.   [*Getting neerer the door still.*

L. Gall. What mean you, Sir? what can my Woman think to see me treated thus?

Sir Char. Well thought on! Nay, we'll do things decently, d'ye see---
Therefore, thou sometimes necessary Utensil, withdraw.   [*Gives her to Sir* Anth.

Sir Anth. Aye, aye, let me alone to teach her her duty. [*Pushes her out, and goes out.*

L. Gall. Stay, *Closet*, I command ye.

---What have you seen in me shou'd move you to this rudeness?   [*To Sir* Char.

Sir Char. No frowning; for by this dear night, 'tis charity, care of your Reputation, Widow: and therefore I am resolv'd nobody shall lie with you but my self.

                                                                                    You

You have dangerous Waſps buzzing about your Hive, Widow---mark that--- [*She flings from him.*] Nay, no parting but upon terms, which in ſhort, d'ye ſee, are theſe: Down on your knees, and ſwear me heartily as Gad ſhall judge your Soul, d'ye ſee, to marry me to morrow.

L. Gall. To morrow ! Oh, I have urgent buſineſs then.

Sir Char. So have I.   Nay Gad, an you be for the neereſt way to wood, the ſober diſcreet way of loving, I am for you, look ye.   [*He begins to undreſs.*

L. Gall. Hold, Sir, what mean you ?

Sir Char. Onely to go to bed, that's all.   [*Still undreſſing.*

L. Gall. Hold, hold, or I'll call out.

Sir Char. Aye do, call up a Jury of your Female Neighbours; they'll be for me, d'ye ſee, bring in the Bill *Ignoramus*, though I am no very true blue Proteſtant neither : Therefore diſpatch, or---

L. Gall. Hold, are you mad ? I cannot promiſe you to night.

Sir Char. Well, well, I'll be content with performance then to night, and truſt you for your promiſe till to morrow.

Sir Anth. [*peeping.*] Ah, Rogue ! By *George*, he out-does my expectations of him.

L. Gall. What Impoſition's this ! I'll call for help.

Sir Char. You need not, you'll do my buſineſs better alone.   [*Pulls her.*

L. Gall. What ſhall I do ! how ſhall I ſend him hence !   [*Aſide.*

Sir Anth. He ſhall ne'er drink ſmall Beer more, that's poſitive : I'll burn all's Books too, they have helpt to ſpoil him ; and ſick or well, ſound or unſound, Drinking ſhall be his Diet, and Whoring his Study.   [*Aſide. Peeping unſeen.*

Sir Char. Come, come, no pauſing ; your promiſe, or I'll to bed.

Offers to pull off his Breeches, having pull'd off almoſt all the reſt of his Clothes.

L. Gall. What ſhall I do, here is no Witneſs neer ! And to be rid of him, I'll promiſe him : he'll have forgot it in his ſober Paſſion.   [*aſide.*

He fumbling to undo his Breeeeches.

Hold, I do ſwear I will---

Sir Char. What ?

L. Gall. Marry you.

Sir Char. When ?

L. Gall. Nay, that's too much.---Hold, hold, I will to morrow. ---Now you are ſatisf'd, you will withdraw?

Enter Sir Anth. *and* Cloſet.

Sir Anth. Charles, Joy *Charles,* give ye Joy : here's two ſubſtantial Witneſſes.

Cloſ. I deny it, Sir ; I heard no ſuch thing.

Sir Anth. What, what, Mrs. *Cloſet,* a Waiting-woman of Honour, and flinch from her Evidence ! Gad, I'll damn thy Soul, if thou dareſt ſwear what thou ſayeſt.

L. Gall. How, upon the catch, Sir ! am I betray'd ?
Baſe and unkind, is this your humble Love !
Is all your whining come to this, falſe man ! By Heaven, I'll be reveng'd.

She goes out in rage, with Cloſet.

Sir Char. Nay, Gad you're caught, ſtruggle and flounder as you pleaſe, Sweetheart, you'll but intangle more ; let me alone to tickle your Gills, i'faith. [*Looking after her.*
---Uncle,

---Uncle, get ye home about your buſineſs : I hope you'll give me the Good morrow, as becomes me.---I ſay no more---A word to the Wiſe---

   Sir Anth. By *George*, thou'rt a brave fellow ; why I did not think it had been in
thee, man.   Well, adieu :   I'll give thee ſuch a Good morrow, *Charles*---the Devil's
in him!---'Buy, *Charles*---a plaguie Rogue!---'Night, Boy---a Divine Youth !
                              Going and returning, as not able to leave him. Exit.

   Sir Char. Gad, I'll not leave her now, till ſhe is mine ;
Then keep her ſo by conſtant conſummation.
Let Man a God do his, I'll do my part,
In ſpight of all her fickleneſs and art ;
There's one ſure way to fix a Widows heart.

ACT the Fifth.

SCENE the Firſt.   *Sir* Timothy's *Houſe.*

Enter Dreſſwell, Fopington, *and five or ſix more diſguiſ'd with Vizards, and dark
  Lanthorns.*

Fop. NOt yet! a Plague of this damn'd Widow : the Devil ow'd him an un-
        lucky Caſt, and has thrown it him to night.
                              Enter Wild. *in Rapture and Joy.*
---Hah, dear *Tom*, art thou come ?
   Wild. I ſaw how at her length ſhe lay !
I ſaw her riſing Boſome bare!
   Fop. A Pox of her riſing Boſome : My Dear, let's dreſs and about our buſineſs.
   Wild. Her looſe thin Robes, through which appear
A Shape deſign'd for Love and Play !
   Dreſſ. 'Sheart, Sir, is this a time for Rapture ? 'tis almoſt day.
   Wild. Ah, *Frank*, ſuch a dear night !
   Dreſſ. A Pox of nights, Sir, think of this and the day to come ; which I perceive
you were too well employ'd to remember.
   Wild. The day to come !
Death, who cou'd be ſo dull in ſuch dear Joys,
To think of time to come, or ought beyond 'em !
And had I not been interrupted by *Charles Meriwill*, who getting drunk, had cou-
rage enough to venture on an untimely Viſit, I'd had no more power of returning, than
committing Treaſon : But that conjugal Lover, who will needs be my Cuckold,
made me then give him way, that he might give it me another time, and ſo unſeen
I got off.   But come---my diſguiſe.   [*Dreſſes.*
   Dreſſ. All's ſtill and huſh, as if Nature meant to favour our deſigne.
                                                                 Wild.

Wild. 'Tis well: And heark ye, my Friends, I'll proscribe you no bounds, or moderation; for I have considered if we modestly take nothing but the Writings, 'twill be easie to suspect the Thief.

Fop. Right; and since 'tis for the securing our Necks, 'tis lawful prize.---Sirrah, leave the Portmantua here.   *Exeunt us into the house.*

After a small time,
Enter Jervice *undrest, crying out, pursu'd by some of the Thieves.*

Jer. Murder, Murder! Thieves, Murder!

Enter Wilding *with his Sword drawn.*

Wild. A Plague upon his Throat; set a Gag in's mouth and bind him, though he be my Uncle's chief Pimp.---So---   [*They bind and gag him.*

Enter Dresswell.

Dress. Well, we have bound all within hearing in their Beds, ere they cou'd alarm their Fellows by crying out.

Wild. 'Tis well: come, follow me, like a kind Midnight-Ghost, I will conduct ye to the rich buried heaps---this door leads to my Uncles Apartment; I know each secred nook contious of Treasure.   [*All go in, leaving* Jervice *bound on the Stage.*

Enter Sensure *running half undrest as from Sir* Timothy's *Chamber, with his Velvet-coat on her shoulders.*

Sen. Help, help! Murder! Murder!   [*Dress.* Laboir, *and others pursue her.*

Dress. What have we here, a Female bolted from Mr. Aldermans Bed?
Holding his Lanthorn to her face.

Sen. Ah mercy, Sir, alas, I am a Virgin.

Dress. A Virgin! Gad and that may be, for any great miracles the old Gentleman can do.

Sen. Do! alas, Sir, I am none of the wicked.

Dress. That's well.---The sanctifi'd Jilt professes Innocence, yet has the Badge of her Occupation about her neck.   [*Pulls off the Coat.*

Sen. Ah misfortune, I have mistook his Worships Coat for my Gown.

A little Book drops out of her Bosome.

Dress. What have we here? *A Sermon preacht by* Richard Baxter, *Divine.* Gad a mercy, Sweetheart, thou art a hopeful Member of the true Protestant Cause.

Sen. Alack, how the Saints may be scandaliz'd! I went but to tuck his Worship in.

Dress. And comment upon the Text a little, which I suppose may be increase and multiply.---Here, gag and bind her.   [*Exit Dress.*

Sen. Hold, hold, I am with Child!

Lab. Then you'll go neer to miscarry of a Babe of Grace.

Enter Wild. Fop. *and others, leading in Sir* Timothy *in his Night-gown and Night-caps.*

Sir Tim. Gentlemen, why Gentlemen, I beseech you use a Conscience in what you do, and have a feeling of what you go about.---Pity my Age.

Wild. Damn'd beggarly Conscience, and needless Pity---

Sir Tim. Oh fearful!---But, Gentlemen, what is't you designe? is it a general Massacar, pray, or am I the onely person aim'd at as a Sacrifice for the Nation? I know, and all the World knows, how many Plots have been laid against my self,

H   both

both by men, women, and children, the Diabolical Emiffaries of the Pope.

Wild. How, Sirrah!   [*Fiercely, he ftarts.*

Sir Tim. Nay, Gentlemen, not but I love and honour his Holinefs with all my Soul ; and if his Grace did but know what I have done for him, d'ye fee—

Fop. You done for the Pope, Sirrah! why what have you done for the Pope?

Sir Tim. Why, Sir, an't like ye, I have done you great fervice, very great fervice : for I have been, d'ye fee, in a fmall Tryal I had, the caufe and occafion of invalidating the Evidence to that degree, that I fuppofe no Jury in *Chriftendom* will ever have the impudence to believe 'em hereafter, fhou'd they fwear againft his Holinefs himfelf, and all the Conclave of Cardinals.

Wild. And yet you plot on ftill, cabal, treat, and keep open debauch, for all the Renegado-Tories and old Commonwealths-men to carry on the good Caufe.

Sir Tim. Alas, what fignifies that ? You know, Gentlemen, that I have fuch a ftrange and natural agility in turning, ---I fhall whip about yet, and leave 'em all in the lurch.

Wild. 'Tis very likely ; but at this time we fhall not take your word for that.

Sir Tim. Bloody minded men, are you refolv'd to affaffinate me then?

Wild. You trifle, Sir, and know our bufinefs better, than to think we come to take your Life, which wou'd not advantage a Dog, much lefs any Party or Perfon.---Come, come, your Keys, your Keys.

Fop. Aye, aye, difcover, difcover your Money, Sir, your ready---

Sir Tim. Money, Sir! good lack, is that all ?   [*Smiling on 'em.*
Why what a Beaft was I, not knowing of your coming, to put out all my Money laft week to Alderman Draw-tooth ! Alack, alack, what fhift fhall I make now to accommodate you ?---But if you pleafe to come again to morrow---

Fop. A fhamming Rogue ; the right Sneer and Grin of a diffembling Whig. Come, come, deliver, Sir ; we are for no Rhetorick, but ready Money.

                                                                Aloud, and threatning.

Sir Tim. Hold, I befeech you, Gentlemen, not fo loud : for there is a Lord, a moft confiderable perfon and a ftranger, honours my houfe to night ; I wou'd not for the world his Lordfhip fhou'd be difturb'd.

Wild. Take no care for him, he's faft bound, and all his Retinue.

Sir Tim. How, bound ! my Lord bound, and all his People ! Undone, undone, difgrac'd ! What will the *Polanders* fay, that I fhou'd expofe their Embaffadour to this difrefpect and affront ?

Wild. Bind him, and take away his Keys.

        They bind him hand and foot, and take his Keys out of his bofome. Exeunt all.

Sir Tim. Aye, aye, what you pleafe, Gentlemen, fince my Lord's bound.---Oh what Recompence can I make for fo unhofpitable ufage ? I am a moft unfortunate Magiftrate !---Hah, who's there, *Jervice ?* Alas, art thou here too? What, canft not fpeak ? But 'tis no matter and I were dumb too : for what Speech or Harangue will ferve to beg my pardon of my Lord ?---And then my Heirefs, *Jervice,* aye, my rich Heirefs, why fhe'll be ravifht, oh Heavens, ravifht ! The young Rogues will have no mercy, *Jervice* ; nay, perhaps as thou fayeft, they'll carry her away.--- Oh that thought ! Gad I'd rather the City-Charter were loft. [*Enter fome with bags of Money.* ---Why Gentlemen, rob like Chriftians, Gentlemen.

                                                                          Fop.

Fop. What, do you mutter, Dog?

Sir Tim. Not in the leaft, Sir, not in the leaft ; onely a Confcience, Sir, in all things does well. ---Barbarous Rogues ! [*They go out all again.*] Here's your Arbitrary Power, *fervice* ; here's the rule of the Sword now for you : Thefe are your Tory Rogues, your Tantivie Royfters ; but we fhall cry quits with you, Rafcals, erelong : and if we do come to our old Trade of Plunder and Sequeftration, we will fo handle ye---we'll fpare neither Prince, Peer, nor Prelate. Oh, I long to have a flice at your fat Church-men, your Crape-Gown-orums.

Enter Wild. *and the reft, with more Bags.*

Wild. A Prize, a Prize, my Lads, in ready Guinies ! Contribution, my Beloved.

Drefs. Nay then 'tis lawful Prize, in fpight of *Ignoramus* and all his Tribe.--- What haft thou there ?   [*To* Fop. *who enters with a bag full of Papers.*

Fop. A whole Bag of Knavery, damn'd Sedition, Libels, Treafon, Succeffions, Rights and Priviledges, with a new-fafhion'd Oath of Abjuration, call'd the Affociation.---Ah Rogue, what will you fay when thefe fhall be made publick ?

Sir Tim. Say, Sir ? why I'll deny it, Sir : for what Jury will believe fo wife a Magiftrate as I, cou'd communicate fuch Secrets to fuch as you ? I'll fay you forg'd 'em, and put 'em in,---or print every one of 'em, and own 'em, as long as they were writ and publifht in *London*, Sir. Come, come, the World is not fo bad yet, but a man may fpeak Treafon within the Walls of *London*, thanks be to God, and honeft confcientious Jury-men. And as for the Money, Gentlemen, take notice you rob the Party.

Wild. Come, come, carry off the Booty, and prithee remove that Rubbifh of the Nation out of the way.---Your Servant, Sir. ---So, away with it to *Dreffwell's* Lodgings, his Coach is at the door ready to receive it.

They carry off Sir Timothy, *and others take up the Bags, and go out with 'em.*

Drefs. Well, you are fure you have all you came for ?

Wild. All's fafe, my Lads, the Writings all---

Fop. Come, let's away then.

Wild. Away ? what meanft thou ? is there not a Lord to be found bound in his bed, and all his People ? Come, come, difpatch, and each man bind his fellow.

Fop. We had better follow the Baggage, Captain.

Wild. No, we have not done fo ill, but we dare fhew our faces. Come, come, to binding.

Fop. And who fhall bind the laft man ?

Wild. Honeft *Laboir*, d'ye hear, Sirrah ? you got drunk and lay in your Clothes under the Hall-table ; d'ye conceive me ? Look to't, ye Rafcal, and carry things difcreetly, or you'll all be hang'd, that's certain.   [*Exit* Wild. *and* Dreff.

Fop. So ; now will I i'th' morning to *Charlot*, and give her fuch a character of her Lover, as if fhe have refentment, makes her mine.   [*Exit* Fop.

Sir Tim. [*calls within.*] Ho, *Jenkin, Roger, Simon* ! where are thefe Rogues ? None left alive to come to my affiftance ? So ho, ho, ho ! Rafcals, Sluggards, Drones ! So ho, ho, ho !

Lab. So, now's my Que---and ftay, I am not yet fober.

Puts himfelf into a drunken pofture.

Sir Tim. Dogs, Rogues, none hear me ? Fire, fire, fire !

Lab. Water, water, I fay : for I am damnable dry.

Sir. Tim. Ha, who's there ?

Lab. What doleful voice is that ?

Sir Tim. What art thou, friend or foe ?   [*In a doleful tone.*

Lab. Very direful---why what the Devil art thou ?

Sir Tim. If thou'rt a friend, approach, approach the wretched.

Lab. Wretched ! What art thou, Ghoft, Hobgobling, or walking Spirit ?
             Reeling in with a Lanthorn in's hand.

Sir Tim. Oh, neither, neither, but meer mortal Sir *Timothy Treat-all*, robb'd and bound.   [*Coming out, led by* Lab.

Lab. How, our generous Hoft ?

Sir Tim. How, one of my Lords Servants ! Alas, alas, how cam'ft thou to efcape ?

Lab. Ene by Miracle, Sir, by being drunk and falling afleep under the Hall-table with your Worfhips Dog *Tory*, till juft now a Dream of Small-beer wakt me ; and crawling from my Kennel to fecure the black Jack, I ftumbled upon this Lanthorn, which I took for one, till I found a Candle in't, which helps me to ferve your Worfhip.   [*Goes to unbind his hands.*

Sir Tim. Hold, hold, I fay ; for I fcorn to be fo uncivil to be unbound before his Lordfhip : therefore run, Friend, to his Honours Chamber, for he, alas, is confin'd too.

Lab. What, and leave his worthy Friend in diftrefs ? by no means, Sir.

Sir Tim. Well then, come, let's to my Lord, whom if I be not afham'd to look in the face, I am an errant Sarazan.   [*Exit Sir* Tim. *and* Lab.

SCENE changes to *Wilding's* Chamber.

He difcover'd fitting in a Chair bound, his Vallet-bound by him ; to them Sir Timothy *and* Laboir.

Wild. Peace, Sirrah ; for fure I hear fome coming.---Villains, Rogues ! I care not for my felf, but the good pious Alderman.   [*Sir* Tim. *as liftening.*

Sir Tim. Wonderful goodnefs, for me ! alas, my Lord, this fight will break my heart.   [*Weeps.*

Wild. Sir *Timothy* fafe ! nay then I do forgive 'em.

Sir Tim. Alas, my Lord, I've heard of your rigid fate.

Wild. It is my cuftom, Sir, to pray an hour or two in my Chamber, before I go to bed ; and having pray'd that drowfie Slave afleep, the Thieves broke in upon us unawares, I having laid my Sword afide.

Sir Tim. Oh, Heavens, at his Prayers ! damn'd Ruffians, and wou'd they not ftay till you had faid your Prayers ?

Wild. By no perfwafion.---Can you not guefs who they fhou'd be, Sir ?

Sir Tim. Oh, fome damn'd Tory-rory Rogues, you may be fure, to rob a man at his Prayers ! Why what will this world come to ?

Wild. Let us not talk, Sir, but purfue 'em.   [*Offering to go.*

Sir Tim. Purfue 'em ? alas, they're paft our reach by this time.

Wild. Oh, Sir, they are neerer than you imagine :

                Some

Some that know each corner of your house, I'll warrant.

Sir Tim. Think ye so, my Lord? Aye, this comes of keeping Open House; which makes so many shut up their doors at Dinner-time.

Enter Dresswell.

Dress. Good morrow, Gentlemen! what was the Devil broke loose to night?

Sir Tim. Onely some of his Imps, Sir, sawcy Varlets, insupportable Rascals.---But well, my Lord, now I have seen your Lordship at liberty, I'll leave you to your rest, and go see what harm this nights work has done.

Wild. I have a little business, Sir, and will take this time to dispatch it in; my Servants shall to bed, though 'tis already day.---I'll wait on you at Dinner.

Sir Tim. Your time: my House and all I have is yours; and so I take my leave of your Lordship. [*Exit Sir* Tim.

Wild. Now for my angry Maid, the young *Charlot*;
'Twill be a task to soften her to peace:
She is all new and gay, young as the Morn,
Blushing as tender Rose-buds on their stalks,
Pregnant with sweets, for the next Sun to ravish.
---Come, thou shalt along with me, I'll trust thy friendship. *Exeunt.*

SCENE changes to *Diana*'s Chamber.

She is discover'd dressing, with Betty.

Dian. Methinks I'm up as early as if I had a mind to what I'm going to do, marry this old rich Coxcomb.

Bet. And you do well to lose no time.

Dian. Ah, *Betty*, and cou'd thy prudence prefer an old Husband, because rich, before so young, so handsome, and so soft a Lover as *Wilding*?

Bet. I know not that, Madam; but I verily believe the way to keep your young Lover, is to marry this old one: for what Youth and Beauty cannot purchase, Money and Quality may.

Dian. Aye, but to be oblig'd to lie with such a Beast; aye, there's the Devil *Betty*. Ah, when I find the difference of their Embraces,
The soft dear Arms of *Wilding* round my neck,
From those cold feeble ones of this old Dotard;
When I shall meet, instead of *Tom*'s warm Kisses,
A hollow pair of thin blue wither'd Lips,
Trembling with Palsie, stinking with Disease,
By Age and Nature baracado'd up
With a kind Nose and Chin;
What fancy or what thought can make my hours supportable?

Bet. What? why six thousand pound a year, Mistriss.
He'll quickly die and leave you rich, and then do what you please.

Dian. Die! no, he's too temperate.---Sure these Whigs, *Betty*, believe there's no Heaven, they take such care to live so long in this world.---No, he'll out-live me. [*Sighs.*
Bet.

Bet. In grace a God he may be hang'd firſt, Miſtriſs.---Ha, one knocks, and I believe 'tis he. *[She goes to open the door.*

Dian. I cannot bring my heart to like this buſineſs;
One ſight of my dear *Tom* wou'd turn the ſcale.

Bet. Who's there?

Enter Sir Tim. *joyful;* Dian. *walks away.*

Sir Tim. 'Tis I, impatient I, who with the Sun have welcom'd in the day;
This happy day to be inroll'd
In Rubrick-letters, and in Gold.

---Hum, I am profoundly eloquent this morning. *[Aſide.*
---Fair Excellence, I approach--- *[Going towards her.*

Dian. Like Phyſick in a morning next one's heart; *[Aſide.*
Which though 'tis neceſſary, is moſt filthy loathſome. *[Going from him.*

Sir Tim. What, do you turn away, bright Sun of Beauty?
---Hum, I'm much upon the Suns and Days this morning. *[Aſide.*

Dian. It will not down. *[Turning to him, looks on him, and turns away.*

Sir Tim. Alas, ye Gods, am I diſpis'd and ſcorn'd?
Did I for this, ponder upon the Queſtion,
Whether I ſhou'd be King or Alderman? *[Heroickly.*

Dian. If I muſt marry him, give him patience to endure the Cuckolding, good
Heaven. *[Aſide.*

Sir Tim. Heaven! did ſhe name Heaven, *Betty?*

Bet. I think ſhe did, Sir.

Sir Tim. I do not like that: What need has ſhe to think of Heaven upon her
Wedding-day?

Dian. Marriage is a ſort of hanging, Sir; and I was onely making a ſhort Prayer
before Execution.

Sir Tim. Oh, is that all? Come, come, we'll let that alone till we are abed, that
we have nothing elſe to do. *[Takes her hand.*

Dian. Not much, I dare ſwear.

Sir Tim. And let us, Fair one, haſte; the Parſon ſtays: beſides, that heap of Scandal may prevent us,---I mean my Nephew.

Dian. A Pox upon him now for naming *Wilding.* *[Weeps.*

Sir Tim. How, weep at naming my ungracious Nephew? Nay, then I am pro-
vokt---Look on this Head, this wiſe and reverend Head; I'd have ye know, it has
been taken meaſure on to fit it to a Crown, d'ye ſee.

Dian. A Halter rather. *[Aſide.*

Sir Tim. Aye, and it fits it too: and am I ſlighted, I that ſhall receive *Billet Deux*
from *Infantas?* 'tis moſt uncivil and impolitick.

Dian. I hope he's mad, and then I reign alone. *[Aſide.*
Pardon me, Sir, that parting Tear I ſhed indeed at naming *Wilding,*
Of whom my fooliſh heart has now tane leave,
And from this moment is intirely yours.

Gives him her hand, they go out.

SCENE

SCENE changes to a Street.

Enter Charlot, *led by* Fopington, *followed by Mrs.* Clacket.

Charl. Stay, my heart misgives me I shall be undone.
—Ah, whither was I going?   [*Pulls her hand from* Fop.

Fop. Do, stay till the news arrives that he is married to her that had his company
to night, my Lady *Galliard*.

Charl. Oh take heed, lest you sin doubly, Sir.

Fop. By Heaven, 'tis true, he past the night with her.

Charl. All night ? what cou'd they find to do ?

Mrs. Clack. A very proper Question : I'll warrant you they were not idle, Madam.

Charl. Oh no ; they lookt and lov'd, and vow'd and lov'd, and swore eternal
Friendship.—Haste, haste, and lead me to the Church, the Altar ; I'll put it past my
power to love him more.

Fop. Oh, how you charm me !   [*Takes her by the hand.*

Charl. Yet what art thou ? a stranger to my heart.
Wherefore, ah why, on what occasion shou'd I ?

Mrs. Clack. Acquaintance, 'tis enough, I know him, Madam, and I hope my word
will be taken for a greater matter i'th' City : In troth you're beholding to the Gentleman for marrying you ; your Reputation's gone.

Charl. How, am I not honest then ?

Mrs. Clack. Marry Heaven forbid ! But who that knows you have been a single
hour in *Wilding's* hands, that wou'd not swear you'd lost your Maidenhead ? And
back again I'm sure you dare not go unmarried ; that wou'd be a fine History to be
sung to your eternal fame in a Ballad.

Fop. Right ; and you see *Wilding* has left you for the Widow, to whom perhaps
you'll shortly hear he's married.

Charl. Oh, you trifle, Sir ; lead on.

          They going out, meet Sir Anthony *with Musick : they return.*

Sir Anth. Come, come, Gentlemen, this is the House, and this the window belong-
ing to my Ladies Bed-chamber : Come, come, let's have some neat, soft, brisk, lan-
guishing, sprightly Air now.

Fop. Old *Meriwill*---how shall I pass by him ?   [*Stand by.*

Sir Anth. So, here's Company too. 'tis very well--Not have the Boy ? I'll warrant
this does the business.---Come, come, screw up your Chitterling.   [*They play.*
---Hold, hold a little,---Good morrow, my Lady *Galliard*,
---Give your Ladyship joy.

Charl. What do I hear, my Lady *Galliard* joy'd ?

Fop. How, married her already ?

Charl. Oh, yes he has. Lovely and false, hast thou deceiv'd my Faith ?

Mrs. Clack. Oh Heavens, Mr. *Fopington*, she faints---ah me !

          They hold her, Musick plays.

                 Enter.

Enter Wilding *and* Dreſſwell *diſguis'd as before.*

Wild. Ah, Muſick at *Galliard's* door!

Sir Anth. Good morrow, Sir *Charles Meriwill ;* give your Worſhip and your fair Lady joy.

Wild. Hah, *Meriwill* married the Widow?

Dreſſ. No matter ; prithee advance and mind thy own affairs.

Wild. Advance, and not inquire the meaning on't!
Bid me not eat, when Appetite invites me ;
Not draw, when branded with the name of Coward ;
Nor love, when Youth and Beauty meets my eyes.---Hah!---

Sees Sir Charles *come into the Belconey undreſt.*

Sir Char. Good-morrow, Uncle. Gentlemen I thank ye : Here, drink the Kings Health, with my Royal Maſter's the Duke.   [*Gives 'em Money.*

Fid. Heaven bleſs your Honour, and your vertuous Bride.

Fop. Wilding ! undone.   [*Shelters* Charlot *that ſhe may not ſee* Wilding.

Wild. Death and the Devil, *Meriwill* above?

Sir Anth. Hah, the Boys Rival here ! By *George,* here may be breathing this morning.---No matter, here's two to two ; come, Gentlemen, you muſt in.

Thruſts the Muſick in, and goes in.

Dreſſ. Is't not what you expected? nay, what you wiſht?

Wild. What then? it comes too ſuddenly upon me---
Ere my laſt kiſs was cold upon her lips,
Before the pantings of her Breaſt were laid,
Rais'd by her Joys with me ; Oh damn'd deluding Woman !

Dreſſ. Be wiſe, and do not ruine where you love.

Wild. Nay, if thou com'ſt to reaſoning, thou haſt loſt me.

Breaks from him and runs in.

Charl. I ſay 'twas *Wilding's* voice, and I will follow it.

Fop. How, Madam, wou'd you after him?

Charl. Nay, force me not : By Heaven I'll cry a Rape,
Unleſs you let me go.---Not after him !
Yes to th'infernal Shades.---Unhand me, Sir.

Fop. How, Madam, have you then deſign'd my ruine?

Charl. Oh, truſt me, Sir, I am a Maid of Honour.   [*Runs in after* Wild.

Mrs. *Clack.* So ; a Murrain of your Projects, we're all undone now : For my part I'll en'e after her, and deny to have any hand in the buſineſs.   [*Goes in.*

Fop. Damn all ill-luck, was ever man thus Fortune-bit, that he ſhou'd croſs my hopes juſt in the nick ? ---But ſhall I loſe her thus? No Gad, I'll after her ; and come the worſt, I have an Impudence ſhall out-face a *Middleſex*-Jury, and out-ſwear a Diſcoverer.   [*Goes in.*

SCENE

SCENE changes to a Chamber.

Enter Lady Galliard *pursued by Sir* Charles, *and Footman.*

L. Gall. Sirrah, run to my Lord Mayors and require some of his Officers to assist me instantly; and d'ye hear, Rascal, bar up my doors, and let none of his mad Crew enter.   [*To the Footman who is going.*

Sir Char. William, you may stay, *William.*

L. Gall. I say, obey me, Sirrah.

Sir Char. Sirrah, I say---know your Lord and Master.

Will. I shall, Sir.   [*Goes out.*

L. Gall. Was ever woman teaz'd thus? pursue me not.

Sir Char. You are mistaken, I'm disobedient grown,
Since we became one Family; and when I've us'd you thus a week or two, you will grow weary of this peevish fooling.

L. Gall. Malicious thing, I wo'not, I am resolv'd I'll tire thee out meerly in spight to have the better of thee.

Sir Char. Gad I'm as resolv'd as you, and do your worst:
For I'm resolv'd never to quit thy house.

L. Gall. But Malice, there are Officers, Magistrates i'th' City, that will not see me us'd thus, and will be here anon.

Sir Char. Magistrates! why they shall be welcome, if they be honest and loyal; if not, they may be hang'd in Heavens good time.

L. Gall. Are you resolv'd to be thus obstinate?
Fully resolv'd to make this way your Conquest?

Sir Char. Most certainly, I'll keep you honest to your word, my Dear, I've Witness---

L. Gall. You will?

Sir Char. You'll find it so.

L. Gall. Then know, if thou darest marry me, I will so plague thee, be so reveng'd for all those tricks thou'st playd me---
---Dost thou not dread the Vengeance Wives can take?

Sir Char. Not at all: I'll trust thy stock of Beauty with thy Wit.

L. Gall. Death, I will cuckold thee.

Sir Char. Why then I shall be free o'th' Reverend City.

L. Gall. Then I will game without cessation, till I've undone thee.

Sir Char. Do, that all the Fops of empty heads and pockets, may know where to be sure of a Cully; and may they rook ye till ye lose, and fret, and chafe, and rail those youthful Eyes to sinking; watch your fair Face to pale and withered leanness.

L. Gall. Then I will never let thee bed with me, but when I please.

Sir Char. For that, see who'll petition first, and then I'll change for new ones every night.

Enter William.

Will. Madam, here's Mr. *Wilding* at the door, and will not be deni'd feeing you.

L. Gall. Hah, *Wilding !* Oh my eternal fhame! now thou haft done thy work.

Sir Char. Now for a ftruggle 'twixt your Love and Honour.

---Yes, here's the Bar to all my Happinefs,
You wou'd be left to the wide World and Love,
To Infamy, to Scandal, and to *Wilding ;*
But I have too much Honour in my Paffion,
To let you loofe to Ruine : Confider and be wife.

L. Gall. Oh, he has toucht my heart too fenfibly.   [*Afide.*

Sir Anth. [*within.*] As far as good Manners goes I'm yours ;
But when you prefs indecently to Ladies Chambers, civil
Queftions ought to be askt, I take it, Sir.

L. Gall. To find him here, will make him mad with Jealoufie, and in the fit he'll
utter all he knows ; Oh, Guilt, what art thou ?   [*Afide.*

Enter Sir Anth. Wild. *and* Dreff.

Dreff. Prithee, dear *Wilding*, moderate thy Paffion.

Wild. By Heaven, I will ; fhe fhall not have the pleafure to fee I am concern'd.
---Morrow, Widow ; you are early up, you mean to thrive I fee, you're like a Mill
that grinds with every Wind.

Sir Char. Hah, *Wilding* this, that paft laft night at Sir *Timothy's* for a man of Quality ? Oh, give him way, *Wilding's* my Friend, my Dear, and now I'm fure I have
the advantage of him in thy love.   I can forgive a hafty word or two.

Wild. I thank thee, *Charles*---What, you are married then ?

L. Gall. I hope you've no exception to my choice.   [*Scornfully.*

Wild. Falfe woman, doft thou glory in thy perfidy ?   [*To her afide angrily.*
---Yes, Faith, I've many exceptions to him   [*Aloud.*
Had you lov'd me, you'd pitcht upon a Blockhead,
Some fpruce gay fool of Fortune, and no more,
Who would have taken fo much care of his own ill-favour'd
Perfon, he fhou'd have had no time to have minded yours,
But left it to the care of fome fond longing Lover.

L. Gall. Death, he will tell him all ! [*afide.*] Oh, you are merry, Sir.

Wild. No, but thou art wonderous falfe,
Falfe as the Love and Joys you feign'd laft night.   [*In a foft tone afide to her.*

L. Gall. Oh, Sir, be tender of thofe treacherous minutes.   [*Softly to him.*
---If this be all you have to fay to me---   [*Walking away, and speaking loud.*

Wild. Faith, Madam, you have us'd me fcurvily,
To marry and not give me notice.   [*Aloud.*
---Curfe on thee, did I onely blow the Fire
To warm another Lover ?   [*To her softly afide.*

L. Gall. Perjur'd---was't not by your advice I marry'd ?
---Oh where was then your Love ?   [*Softly to him afide.*

Wild. So foon did I advife,
Didft thou invite me to the Feaft of Love,
To fnatch away my Joys as foon as tafted ;

Ah.

Ah, where was then your Modesty and sense of Honour?   [*Aside to her in a low tone.*

L. Gall. Aye, where indeed, when you so quickly vanquisht?   [*Soft.*

---But you I find are come prepar'd to rail.   [*Aloud.*

Wild. No, 'twas with thee to make my last effort against your scorn.

                          Shews her the Writings.

And this I hop'd, when all my Vows and Love,

When all my Languishments cou'd nought prevail,

Had made ye mine for ever.   [*Aloud.*

        Enter Sir Anthony *pulling in Sir* Timothy *and* Diana.

Sir Anth. 'Morrow, *Charles*, 'Morrow to your Ladyship: *Charles*, bid Sir *Timothy* welcome; I met him luckily at the door, and am resolv'd none of my Friends shall pass this joyful day without giving thee Joy, *Charles*, and drinking my Ladies Health.

Wild. Hah, my Uncle here so early?   [*Aside.*

Sir Tim. What has your Ladyship serv'd me so? How finely I had been mumpt now, if I had not took heart a grace and shew'd your Ladyship trick for trick: for I have been this morning about some such business of Life too, Gentlemen; I am married to this fair Lady, the Daughter and Heiress of Sir *Nicholas Gettall*, Knight and Alderman.

Wild. Hah, married to *Diana*!

How fickle is the Faith of common women?   [*Aside.*

Sir Tim. Hum, Who's here, my Lord? What, I see your Lordship has found the way already to the fair Ladies; but I hope your Lordship will do my Wedding-dinner the honour to grace it with your presence.

Wild. I shall not fail, Sir.

A Pox upon him, he'll discover all.   [*Aside.*

L. Gall. I must own, Sir *Timothy*, you have made the better choice.

Sir Tim. I cou'd not help my destiny; Marriages are made in Heaven, you know.

        Enter Charlot *weeping, and* Clacket.

Charl. Stand off, and let me loose as are my Griefs, which can no more be bounded: Oh let me face the perjur'd, false, forsworn!

L. Gall. Fair Creature, who is't that you seek with so much sorrow?

Charl. Thou, thou fatally fair Inchantress.   [*Weeps.*

Wild. *Charlot*! Nay then I am discover'd.

L. Gall. Alas, what wou'dst thou?

Charl. That which I cannot have, thy faithless Husband.

Be judge, ye everlasting Powers of Love,

Whether he more belongs to her or me.

Sir Anth. How, my Nephew claim'd? Why how now, Sirrah, have you been dabling here?

Sir Char. By Heaven, I know her not.---Heark ye, Widow, this is some trick of yours, and 'twas well laid: and Gad, she's so pretty, I cou'd find in my heart to take her at her word.

L. Gall. Vile man, this will not pass your falshood off.

Sure 'tis some Art to make me jealous of him,

To find how much I value him.

                I 2   *Sir*

Sir Char. Death, I'll have the forgery out ;
---Tell me, thou pretty weeping Hypocrite, who was it set thee on to lay a claim to me ?

Charl. To you! Alas, who are you ? for till this moment I never saw your face.

L. Gall. Mad as the Seas when all the Winds are raging.

Sir Tim. Aye, aye, Madam, stark mad ! Poor Soul---Neighbour, pray let her lie i'th' dark, d'ye hear.

Sir Char. How came you, pretty one, to lose your Wits thus ?

Charl. With loving, Sir, strongly, with too much loving.
---Will you not let me see the lovely false one ? 　　　　　　　　　　　[*To* L. Gall.
For I am told you have his heart in keeping.

L. Gall. Who is he ? pray describe him.

Charl. A thing just like a Man, or rather Angel !
He speaks, and looks, and loves, like any God !
All fine and gay, all manly, and all sweet :
And when he swears he loves, you wou'd swear too
That all his Oaths were true.

Sir Anth. Who is she ? some one who knows her and is wiser, speak---you, Mistris. 　　　　　　　　　[*To* Clacket.

Mrs. Clack. Since I must speak, there comes the man of Mischief :
---'Tis you I mean, for all your leering, Sir. 　　　　　　　　　[*To* Wild.

Wild. So.

Sir Tim. What, my Lord !

Mrs. Clack. I never knew your Nephew was a Lord : Has his Honour made him forget his Honesty ? 　　　　　　　[Charl. *runs and catches him in her Arms.*

Charl. I have thee, and I'll die thus grasping thee :
Thou art my own, no Power shall take thee from me.

Wild. Never, thou truest of thy Sex, and dearest,
Thou soft, thou kind, thou constant Sufferer,
This moment end thy fears ; for I am thine.

Charl. May I believe thou art not married then ?

Wild. How can I, when I'm yours ?
How cou'd I, when I love thee more than Life ?
---Now, Madam, I'm reveng'd on all your scorn. 　　　　　　　[*To* L. Gall.
---And, Uncle, all your cruelty.

Sir Tim. Why, what are you indeed my Nephew, *Thomas* ?

Wild. I am *Tom Wilding*, Sir, that once bore some such Title, till you discarded me, and left me to live upon my Wits.

Sir Tim. What, and are you no Polish Embassadour then incognito ?

Wild. No, Sir, nor you no King Elect, but must e'en remain as you were ever, Sir, a most seditious pestilent old Knave ; one that deludes the Rabble with your Politicks, then leave 'em to be hang'd, as they deserve, for silly mutinous Rebels.

Sir Tim. I'll peach the Rogue, and then he'll be hang'd in course, because he's a Tory. One comfort is, I have couzen'd him of his rich Heiress ; for I am married, Sir, to Mrs. *Charlot.*

Wild. Rather *Diana*, Sir ; I wish you Joy : See here's *Charlot* ! I was not such a Fool to trust such Blessings with the Wicked.

　　　　　　　　　　　　　　　　　　　　　　　　　　　　　　　Sir

Sir Char. How, Mrs. *Dy* Ladyfi'd! This is an excellent way of disposing an old cast-off Mistrifs.

Sir Tim. How, have I married a Strumpet then?

Diah. You give your Nephew Mistrifs, Sir, too coarfe a name: 'Tis true, I lov'd him, onely him, and was true to him.

Sir Tim. Undone, undone! I shall ne'r make *Guildhall*-speech more; but he shall hang for't, if there be one a Witness to be had between this and *Salamancha* for Money.

Wild. Do your worst, Sir; Witnesses are out of fashion now, Sir, thanks to your *Ignoramus* Juries!

Sir Tim. Then I'm resolv'd to dif-inherit him.

Wild. See, Sir, that's past your skill too, thanks to my laft nights Ingenuity: they're [*shews him the Writings*] fign'd, feal'd, and deliver'd in the prefence of, &c.

Sir Tim. Bear Witness, 'twas he that robb'd me laft night.

Sir Anth. We bear Witness, Sir, we know of no such matter we. I thank you for that, Sir, wou'd you make Witnesses of Gentlemen?

Sir Tim. No matter for that, I'll have him hang'd, nay drawn and quarter'd.

Wild. What, for obeying your Commands, and living on my Wits?

Sir Anth. Nay, then 'tis a cleer cafe you can neither hang him nor blame him.

Wild. I'll propofe fairly now, if you'll be generous and pardon all: I'll render your Eftate back during Life, and put the Writings in Sir *Anthony Meriwill's* and Sir *Charles* his hands.---

I have a Fortune here that will maintain me,
Without fo much as wifhing for your death.

All. This is but Reafon.

Sir Char. With this Provifo, that he makes not ufe on't to promote any mifchief to the King and Government.

All. Good and juft.　　　　　　　　　　　　　　　　[*Sir* Tim. *paufes.*

Sir Tim. Hum, I'd as good quietly agree to't, as lofe my Credit by making a noife. ---Well, *Tom*, I pardon all, and will be Friends.　　　[*Gives him his hand.*

Sir Char. See, my dear Creature, even this hard old man is mollifi'd at laft into good nature; yet you'll ftill be cruel.

L. Gall. No, your unwearied Love at laft has vanquifht me. Here, be as happy as a Wife can make ye---One laft look more, and then---be gone fond Love.

　　　　　　Sighing and looking on Wilding, *giving Sir* Charles *her hand.*

Sir Char. Come, Sir, you muft receive *Diana* too; fhe is a cheerful witty Girl, and handfome, one that will be a Comfort to your Age, and bring no fcandal home. Live peaceably, and do not trouble your decrepid Age with bufinefs of State.

　　　　Let all things in their own due order move;
　　　　Let *Cæfar* be the Kingdoms care and love:
　　　　Let the Hot-headed Mutineers petition,
　　　　And meddle in the Rights of Juft Succeffion;
　　　　But may all honeft hearts as one agree
　　　　To blefs the King, and Royal *Albanie.*

THE END.

EPILOGUE,

Written by a Person of Quality.

SPOKEN by Mrs. BOTELER.

MY Part, I fear, will take with but a few,
   A rich young Heireſs to her firſt Love true!
'Tis damn'd unnatural, and paſt enduring,
Againſt the fundamental Laws of Whoring.
Marrying's the Mask, which Modeſty aſſures,
Helps to get new, and covers old Amours;
And Husband ſounds ſo dull to a Town-Bride,
You now-a-days condemn him ere he's try'd;
Ere in his Office he's confirm'd Poſſeſſor,
Like Trincaloes you chuſe him a Succeſſor,
In the gay ſpring of Love, when free from doubts,
With early ſhoots his Velvet Forehead ſprouts.
Like a poor Parſon bound to hard Indentures,
You make him pay his Firſt-fruits ere he enters.
But for ſhort Carnivals of ſtoln good Cheer,
You're after forc'd to keep Lent all the Year;
Till brought at laſt to a ſtarving Nuns condition,
You break into our Quarters for Proviſion:
Invade Fop-corner with your glaring Beauties,
And tice our Loyal Subjects from their Duties.
Pray, Ladies, leave that Province to our care;
A Fool is the Fee-ſimple of a Player,   }
In which we Women claim a double ſhare.

EPILOGUE.

In other things the Men are Rulers made ;
But catching Woodcocks is our proper Trade.
If by Stage-Fops they a poor Living get,
We can grow rich, thanks to our Mother Wit,
By the more natural Blockheads in the Pit.
Take then the Wits, and all their useless Prattles ;
But as for Fools, they are our Goods and Chattels.
Return, Ingrates, to your first Haunt the Stage;
We taught your Youth, and help'd your feeble Age.
What is't you see in Quality we want ?
What can they give you which we cannot grant ?
We have their Pride, their Frolicks, and their Paint.
We feel the same Youth dancing in our Blood ;
Our dress as gay----All underneath as good.
Most men have found us hitherto more true,
And, if we're not abus'd by some of you,
We're full as fair----perhaps as wholesome too.
But if at best our hopeful Sport and Trade is,
And nothing now will serve you but great Ladies ;
May question'd Marriages your Fortune be,.
And Lawyers drain your Pockets more than we :
May Judges puzzle a clear Case with Laws,
And Musquetoon at last decide the Cause.

FINIS.

In other things the Men are Rulers made;
But catching Woodcocks is our proper Trade.
We're full as fair----perhaps as wholesome too.
And nothing now will serve you but great Ladies.
And Lawyers drain your Pockets more than we;
May Judges puzzle a clear Cafe with Laws,
And Mulquetoon at laft decide the Caufe.

FINIS.

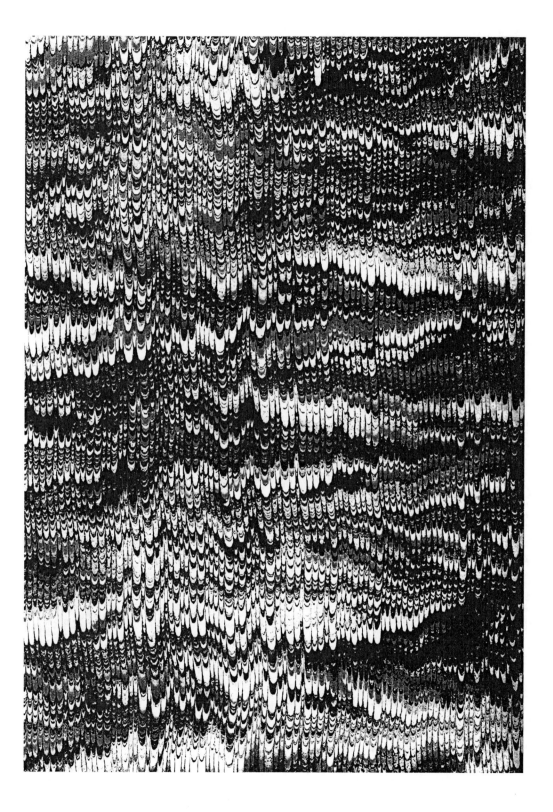

CPSIA information can be obtained at www.ICGtesting.com
Printed in the USA
LVOW081641310712

292376LV00005B/54/P